MANHATTAN GMAT

Integrated Reasoning & Essay

GMAT Strategy Guide

This guide covers the Integrated Reasoning and Essay sections on the GMAT. Master advanced new question types, and discover strategies for optimizing performance on the essay.

guide **9**

Integrated Reasoning & Essay GMAT Strategy Guide, Fifth Edition

10-digit International Standard Book Number: 1-935707-83-3
13-digit International Standard Book Number: 978-1-935707-83-7
eISBN: 978-1-937707-10-1

Note: *GMAT, Graduate Management Admission Test, Graduate Management Admission
Council,* and *GMAC* are all registered trademarks of the Graduate Management Admission
Council, which neither sponsors nor is affiliated in any way with this product.

Layout Design: Dan McNaney and Cathy Huang
Cover Design: Evyn Williams and Dan McNaney
Cover Photography: Alli Ugosoli

SUSTAINABLE FORESTRY INITIATIVE

Certified Chain of Custody
Promoting Sustainable Forestry
www.sfiprogram.org
SFI-00756

INSTRUCTIONAL GUIDE SERIES

SUPPLEMENTAL GUIDE SERIES

MANHATTAN
GMAT

April 24th, 2012

Dear Student,

Thank you for picking up a copy of *Integrated Reasoning & Essay*. I hope this book provides just the guidance you need to get the most out of your GMAT studies.

As with most accomplishments, there were many people involved in the creation of the book you are holding. First and foremost is Zeke Vanderhoek, the founder of Manhattan GMAT. Zeke was a lone tutor in New York when he started the company in 2000. Now, 12 years later, the company has instructors and offices nationwide and contributes to the studies and successes of thousands of students each year.

Our Manhattan GMAT Strategy Guides are based on the continuing experiences of our instructors and students. For this volume, we are particularly indebted to Liz Ghini-Moliski, Dave Mahler, and Stacey Koprince. Dave deserves special recognition for his contributions over the past number of years. Dan McNaney and Cathy Huang provided their design expertise to make the books as user-friendly as possible, and Noah Teitelbaum and Liz Krisher made sure all the moving pieces came together at just the right time. And there's Chris Ryan. Beyond providing additions and edits for this book, Chris continues to be the driving force behind all of our curriculum efforts. His leadership is invaluable. Finally, thank you to all of the Manhattan GMAT students who have provided input and feedback over the years. This book wouldn't be half of what it is without your voice.

At Manhattan GMAT, we continually aspire to provide the best instructors and resources possible. We hope that you will find our commitment manifest in this book. If you have any questions or comments, please email me at dgonzalez@manhattanprep.com. I'll look forward to reading your comments, and I'll be sure to pass them along to our curriculum team.

Thanks again, and best of luck preparing for the GMAT!

Sincerely,

Dan Gonzalez
President
Manhattan GMAT

HOW TO ACCESS YOUR ONLINE RESOURCES

If you...

⊙ are a registered Manhattan GMAT student

and have received this book as part of your course materials, you have AUTOMATIC access to ALL of our online resources. This includes all practice exams, question banks, and online updates to this book. To access these resources, follow the instructions in the Welcome Guide provided to you at the start of your program. Do NOT follow the instructions below.

⊙ purchased this book from the Manhattan GMAT online store or at one of our centers

1. Go to: http://www.manhattangmat.com/practicecenter.cfm.

2. Log in using the username and password used when your account was set up.

⊙ purchased this book at a retail location

1. Create an account with Manhattan GMAT at the website: https://www.manhattangmat.com/createaccount.cfm.

2. Go to: http://www.manhattangmat.com/access.cfm.

3. Follow the instructions on the screen.

Your one year of online access begins on the day that you register your book at the above URL.

You only need to register your product ONCE at the above URL. To use your online resources any time AFTER you have completed the registration process, log in to the following URL: http://www.manhattangmat.com/practicecenter.cfm.

Please note that online access is nontransferable. This means that only NEW and UNREGISTERED copies of the book will grant you online access. Previously used books will NOT provide any online resources.

⊙ purchased an eBook version of this book

1. Create an account with Manhattan GMAT at the website: https://www.manhattangmat.com/createaccount.cfm.

2. Email a copy of your purchase receipt to books@manhattangmat.com to activate your resources. Please be sure to use the same email address to create an account that you used to purchase the eBook.

For any technical issues, email books@manhattangmat.com or call 800-576-4628.

Please refer to the following page for a description of the online resources that come with this book.

YOUR ONLINE RESOURCES

Your purchase includes ONLINE ACCESS to the following:

 ### 6 Computer-Adaptive Online Practice Exams

The 6 full-length computer-adaptive practice exams included with the purchase of this book are delivered online using Manhattan GMAT's proprietary computer-adaptive test engine. The exams adapt to your ability level by drawing from a bank of more than 1,200 unique questions of varying difficulty levels written by Manhattan GMAT's expert instructors, all of whom have scored in the 99th percentile on the Official GMAT. At the end of each exam you will receive a score, an analysis of your results, and the opportunity to review detailed explanations for each question. You may choose to take the exams timed or untimed.

The content presented in this book is updated periodically to ensure that it reflects the GMAT's most current trends and is as accurate as possible. You may view any known errors or minor changes upon registering for online access.

Important Note: The 6 computer adaptive online exams included with the purchase of this book are the SAME exams that you receive upon purchasing ANY book in the Manhattan GMAT Complete Strategy Guide Set.

Integrated Reasoning & Essay Online Question Banks

The Bonus Online Question Banks for *Integrated Reasoning & Essay* consists of extra practice questions (with detailed explanations) that test the variety of concepts and skills covered in this book. These questions provide you with extra practice beyond the problem sets contained in this book. You may use our online timer to practice your pacing by setting time limits for each question in the banks.

Online Updates to the Contents in this Book

The content presented in this book is updated periodically to ensure that it reflects the GMAT's most current trends. You may view all updates, including any known errors or changes, upon registering for online access.

TABLE *of* CONTENTS

guide **9**

Chapter 1 of Integrated Reasoning

Introduction to Integrated Reasoning

In This Chapter...

Chapter 1:
Introduction to Integrated Reasoning

The new Integrated Reasoning section of the GMAT launches in June 2012. The "IR" section replaces one of the two essays at the beginning of the test. Like an essay, Integrated Reasoning takes 30 minutes, so the whole exam takes the same amount of time as before.

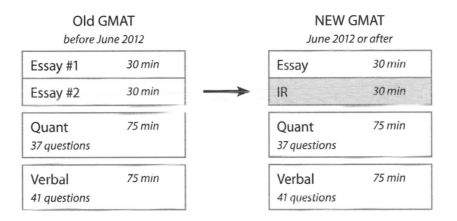

As the name implies, Integrated Reasoning asks you to do **both math and verbal thinking** as you answer questions based on 12 prompts, or sets of information for you to analyze. Many prompts and questions have new, unfamiliar formats.

IR is separately scored. Your performance on IR does not affect your score on any other section. The IR scoring system will be finalized by April 2012. Check our site for updates.

1

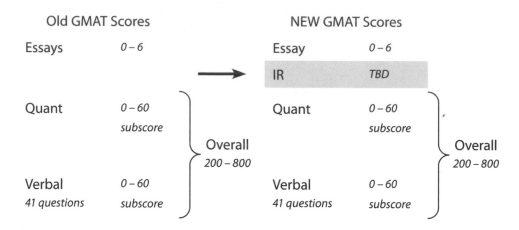

How schools will interpret the results is somewhat uncertain. Most likely, admissions officers will put only *moderate* weight on the IR score at first. Don't count on them ignoring the score altogether, but at least initially, an IR result will probably be interpreted as just another piece of data, one additional element in an applicant's mosaic.

Over time, admissions officers will observe how performance on the IR section correlates with academic performance in business school. The predictive power of the IR score can't be entirely known in advance. Thus, the role and importance of IR in the admissions process will not be completely clear for some time.

The Purpose of the IR Section

Most business schools use **case studies** to teach some or even most topics. Cases are true histories of difficult business situations: they include vast amounts of real information, both quantitative and verbal, that you must sort through and analyze to glean insights and make decisions.

The old GMAT has been a decent predictor of academic success in business school; thus, it must measure the quant and verbal skills required for case analysis.

What the old GMAT could *not* fully do is mirror two key aspects of case analysis: **math-verbal integration** and the **flood of real-world data**. The IR section puts a new, unique focus on these aspects.

Of course, any word problem on GMAT Quant involves math-verbal integration, and a few Critical Reasoning questions require you to draw numeric conclusions. However, you never have to apply hard quantitative thinking to numbers embedded in a Reading Comprehension passage. On the IR section, you will have to do such thinking.

Likewise, real-world data in excess quantity is new to the GMAT. In fact, current Quant problems include extraneous information so rarely that you can often break logjams by asking yourself what data you *haven't* used yet. Moreover, the numbers in the Quant section are rigged for easy computation by hand, once you see the trick.

In contrast, Integrated Reasoning gives you giant tables of ugly numbers, many of which you'll never compute with. And you'll need to use the provided calculator to save time as you crunch messy decimals.

It is true that Reading Comprehension passages include lots of miscellaneous facts that you won't be asked about, but IR takes this fun feature to the next level.

In short, the new IR section seeks to measure your ability to do **case analysis** in business school.

How? By asking you to do **mini-case analysis on the GMAT**.

Integrated Reasoning is very "business-school"-like, so it might seem that admissions officers would pay particular attention to the score.

Remember two things, though: IR is brand-new, and it's only 30 minutes long.

We believe that for a significant period of time at minimum, your performance on the standard Quant and Verbal sections (the 200–800 score) will be substantially more important than your performance on IR.

Don't Let IR Mess Up the Rest of Your Test

Unfortunately, for most people the Integrated Reasoning section is much harder than the Issue essay that it replaces. You have to absorb a ton of new data of various types, repeatedly shift mental gears, and make a swarm of decisions… all in 30 minutes.

Twelve data-intensive prompts, with at least one question per prompt, in just 30 minutes?

That's some *intense* time pressure. You will have to work fast and avoid rat holes. Most importantly— you will have to recover very quickly for the rest of the exam.

Unfortunately, after the IR section, your brain will be spent. How should you prepare to deal with this mental exhaustion? Do the following:

- **Build stamina in advance.** Take more than one full practice exam with the IR section included.
- During review, **study the fast and *easy* way** to do each problem. Then drill that way into your head. Don't be too cool to use the calculator.
- **Replenish your brain's food**—glucose. During the break after IR, drink Gatorade or a similar energy drink. Nothing else will work faster to counter so-called "decision fatigue" and restore your mental willpower. As you go to your locker, only get a beverage or an energy bar. Do not touch your cell phone or anything else—your exam will be immediately disqualified if you do.

IR can mess up the rest of your test in another way. Coming out of IR, you will have to make a couple of small but critical adjustments to the way you solve quant and verbal problems.

Think of roller skates and roller blades. You accelerate and turn on them basically the same way, but you stop differently. In fact, the similarity of roller skates and roller blades can be dangerous, if you mix up which ones you're zooming around on.

The new GMAT makes you wear roller skates for IR, then switch to roller blades for Quant and Verbal. Be aware of the following differences, so you don't wipe out!

GMAT Quant

As you go from Integrated Reasoning to the Quant section, you have to switch from using a calculator to estimating or applying other computation tricks.

On IR, you *should* use the calculator, because IR questions sometimes demand that you make computations with nasty numbers to within 10–15% of the right answer. Why waste time and energy estimating when you have a calculator handy? (Of course, don't turn off your number sense; it's nice to spot ridiculous results that come from keystroke errors.)

When you move to the Quant section, the calculator is taken away. It feels worse to lose something you once had, but *avoid getting frustrated*. Just remember that the numbers are now rigged. There must be a shortcut through estimation or some other method that you can apply by hand.

You must also switch from **ignoring extra data** to **never ignoring data**.

On IR, you have to sift through mounds of given information. To do so quickly, you have to see *what kind* of information you're given, but you should not read every last digit carefully.

On GMAT Quant, you are *almost never* given unnecessary information. Even long word problems avoid providing extraneous facts. When you get stuck, you should check to see that you've used everything given to you.

GMAT Verbal

When you get to the Verbal section, you have to stop reading between the lines. On Integrated Reasoning, you sometimes have to make very *subtle* inferences from real-world communications, such as email exchanges. Dialogues of any kind are very rare in Verbal, but they occur with some regularity in the IR section.

As you interpret a dialogue, you have to infer the mindsets of the speakers or writers from what is said, how it is said, and even what is *not* said. You also have to pick up on how these mindsets may change as the dialogue progresses. This sort of IR content reflects social relationships, much like a scene in a play or on TV.

In contrast, on GMAT Verbal you read plain text: expository passages and arguments. The mindset of the author is much simpler to interpret. In fact, you should turn off the ear for social nuances that you had activated for IR. **Avoid reading too much into the text on Verbal.** Stay close to the actual words on the screen.

In both IR and Verbal, the precise use of language matters a great deal. But in IR, the textual proof can be implicit, and you'll need to be sensitive to social context. On Verbal, there's little social context, and the proof is made more explicit.

Integrated Reasoning in Detail

The Integrated Reasoning section contains 12 prompts, each associated with one or more questions (just as Reading Comprehension passages are). You will almost certainly not be asked more than three questions for any given prompt.

There are four types of prompts. Note that the first two types are interactive:

1. Multi-Source Reasoning
Switch between two or three tabs of information.

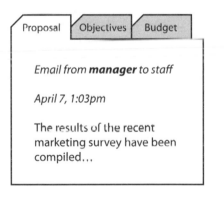

Interactive

2. Table Analysis
Sort a table by any column using a pull-down menu.

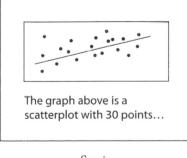

Interactive

3. Graphics Interpretation
Interpret a graph or other image.

The graph above is a scatterplot with 30 points…

Static

4. Two-Part Analysis
Answer a two-part question.

Here is some information.

*The format of this prompt is not interesting. However, the question type associated with this prompt **is** interesting.*

Static

There are also four types of questions you can be asked: traditional multiple-choice and three new types that demand two or more responses per question.

A. Traditional Multiple Choice

Pick one of five choices, as usual.

What is the increase… ?

- ○ 10%
- ● 20%
- ○ 30%
- ○ 40%
- ○ 50%

B. Either/Or Statements*

Choose one side or the other for each of three statements.

True	False	
○	●	Statement 1
●	○	Statement 2
○	●	Statement 3

C. Drop-Down Statements

Make one choice from a drop-down menu for each of two statements.

The slope is [positive ▼].

The volume is [Select... ▼].
- 100 cc
- 200 cc
- 300 cc
- 400 cc

D. Two-Part Question

Make one choice in each of two columns.

Co. A	Co. B	Profit
○	○	−$200 million
○	○	−$100 million
○	●	$0
○	○	$100 million
●	○	$200 million
○	○	$300 million

Don't let these fancy question types throw you. They're just slightly different "looks." In all cases, you simply answer the question you're asked.

What really makes these new types harder is that you have to give **two or more responses per question**. This means you have to move *even faster* to get through them. It is likely that the GMAT will award partial credit in some fashion.

Also, don't mix up Either/Or Statements with Two-Part Questions. With Either/Or Statements, you make one choice in each *row*. With Two-Part Questions, you make one choice in each *column*.

---

* The GMAT calls this type "multiple-dichotomous choice." We figured we'd come up with a nicer name.

Here's how the prompts and question types match up:

Prompt	**Question**	**Questions per Prompt**

1. Multi-Source Reasoning   **A. Traditional Multiple Choice**

Email from **manager** to staff April 7, 1:03pm The results of the recent marketing survey have been compiled...	What is the increase... ? ○ 10% ● 20% ○ 30% ○ 40% ○ 50%	Probably 1

B. Either/Or Statements

	True False ○ ● Statement 1 ● ○ Statement 2 ○ ● Statement 3	Probably 2 3 statements = 3 responses (1 per row)

2. Table Analysis   **B. Either/Or Statements**

Sort by [Select ▼]		
City	Population	3–7 more columns
Alphaville	412,390	...
Baskerville	287,840	...
Camelot	123,050	...
4–20 more rows		

True False ○ ● Statement 1 ● ○ Statement 2 ○ ● Statement 3	Just 1 per prompt 3 statements = 3 responses (1 per row)

3. Graphics Interpretation   **C. Drop-Down Statements**

The graph above is a scatterplot with 30 points...	The slope is [positive ▼] . The volume is [Select... ▼] . 100 cc 200 cc 300 cc 400 cc

Just 1 per prompt
2 responses (1 per statement)

4. Two-Part Analysis   **D. Two-Part Question**

Here is some information. *The format of this prompt is not interesting. However, the question type associated with this prompt is interesting.*	Co. A Co. B Profit ○ ○ –$200 million ○ ○ –$100 million ○ ● $0 ○ ○ $100 million ● ○ $200 million ○ ○ $300 million

Just 1 per prompt
2 responses (1 per column. Note: The same answer could be right for *both* columns!)

Unlike the Quant and Verbal sections, IR is **not adaptive**: it does not get harder or easier, depending on how you answer. As you proceed through the IR section, you **cannot go back to earlier questions**.

The relative composition of the IR section—how many prompts of each type, how many questions of each type—is still not certain as this book goes to press. It is likely that there will be *fewer interactive* prompts (Multi-Source Reasoning and Table Analysis) than *static* prompts (Graphics Interpretation and Two-Part Analysis), since the interactive prompts are more complex and time-consuming to deal with. Again, check the website for updates.

The Calculator

A simple calculator is available to you at all times on Integrated Reasoning.

Click the Calculator link in the upper left corner of the window. The calculator floats above the question and disables it temporarily. You can drag the calculator anywhere on the screen.

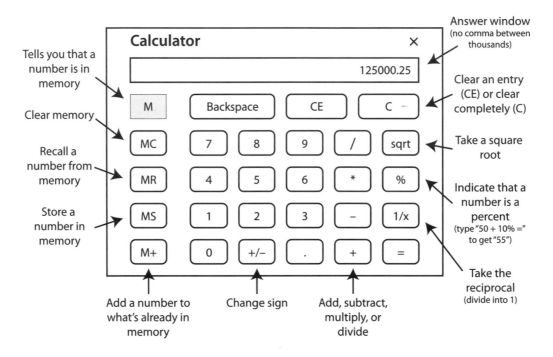

You can click buttons with your mouse or use the keyboard, once you've clicked in the answer window. Not every button has a keyboard equivalent—only the numbers, arithmetic operations, backspace, decimal point, and percent sign. The equals sign (=) works, but not the Enter key.

The calculator is not a luxury. IR problems force you to make fast calculations with messy numbers. Practice using the calculator and plan to use it on the exam to avoid mental fatigue, which leads to silly errors. Write or sketch out your math on paper first, so that you execute the right operations.

Chapter 2 *of* Integrated Reasoning

IR Quant

In This Chapter...

Chapter 2:

IR Quant

The math side of the Integrated Reasoning section differs from that of the GMAT Quant in a few subtle but important ways. Exaggerating the differences a bit, we can describe the Integrated Reasoning as "real world," while GMAT Quant is more based on "math tricks."

Integrated Reasoning – *Real World*	GMAT Quant – *Math Tricks*
Numbers are **ugly**, as if from the **real world**. The **calculator** provided on-screen is useful, even necessary. Results are sometimes "real," as if to answer a business question. *Example:* $0.478 billion $\div$ 0.763% = ? $= 0.478 \div 0.00763$ $= \$62.7$ billion	Numbers are rigged. Once you see how, you can manipulate them nicely. No calculator is provided—or needed. Results are often artificial, like those for a math puzzle. *Example:* $3^{17} - 3^{16} + 3^{15} = ?$ $= 3^{15}(9 - 3 + 1)$ $= 3^{15}(7)$
Extra information is often provided. You must sift the data to find what's relevant. *Example:* In the following big table, how many cities have both > 3% job growth and < 8% unemployment? *Many cities in the table won't fit.*	Extra information is rarely provided. If you didn't use everything, you probably made a mistake. Your task is to follow a chain of deductions. *Example:* $x < y < z$ but $x^2 > y^2 > z^2$, which of the following must be positive? *Use all the constraints given.*
Necessary data is provided in **many different forms**, such as tables and charts. Numbers can be embedded in lots of descriptive text.	Tables and charts are provided infrequently. Numbers are embedded in smaller quantities of text, such as short word problems.

2

In short, you have a lot of ugly numbers, graphical data, and text. You've got a calculator, but not a lot of time.

What does all this mean? A blessing in disguise:

- They *can't* ask for anything that takes a long time to compute.
- IR math will be more focused than the GMAT Quant section. Topics such as percents will be emphasized at the expense of other topics, such as number properties and geometry.

So, how do you deal with IR math?

First and foremost, prepare for GMAT Quant. All the practice that you are doing with word problems and FDP questions (Fractions, Decimals, and Percents) is perfectly applicable here. You are killing two birds with one stone.

Second, you need a good problem-solving process.

How to Tackle IR Quant: Understand-Plan-Solve

Here is a universal four-step process for Integrated Reasoning math:

1. Understand the prompt.
2. Understand the question.
3. Plan your approach.
4. Solve the problem.

This process works well for GMAT Quant, too (although those prompts are shorter, so you can usually combine steps 1 and 2).

If you are already comfortable with reading charts and manipulating information from them, you can be more relaxed about this process. However, you should not discard it entirely. A simple, structured checklist reduces the likelihood of a disaster if something unexpected happens.

Airline pilots, fire fighters, and emergency medical personnel have ultra-clear processes for dealing with stressful situations. You should as well.

1. Understand the Prompt

As you scan the given data, ask yourself "What and So What":

- **What** is this?
- **So What** about this?

"What is this?" directs your attention:

- What is in this chart, this row, or this column?
- What do these points represent? Read titles and labels.
- What kind of graph is this—pie, column, line, bubble, etc.?
- What kind of numbers are these—percents, ranks, or absolute quantities, such as dollars or barrels?
- Don't forget to glance over accompanying text. Valuable totals or other numbers can be buried in footnotes.

"So What about this?" keeps you thinking about the big picture:

- How is this information organized? How does it all fit together? Draw connections.
- Why is this part here? What purpose does it serve, relative to everything else?
- Note key similarities and differences, but do not try to master detail.

You might be tempted to skip this "understand the prompt" step and jump into answering the question. But the time you take to scan the data and understand it will help you to solve the problem faster—and better.

2. Understand the Question

Take your time reading the question before you try to solve it. What are they asking for *precisely*? The wording can trick you. For instance, you might think that you must use an advanced, time-consuming technique, or that you need information that you really don't need.

You may hear the clock ticking away, but don't let it panic you. No one can solve these problems without taking time up front, including Manhattan GMAT instructors. If you don't spend the time, you might chase an illusory rabbit down a rabbit hole. We know. We've chased that rabbit before, too!

3. Plan Your Approach

Just as on GMAT Quant, think about different ways to solve the problem. One way is usually easier than all the others—look for it.

Many methods work similarly for both IR math and GMAT Quant:

- Reorganize and plan on paper:
  - With IR math, you won't want to copy *everything* down, but don't try to figure too much out in your head.
  - Translate the work to specific tasks. For tricky computations on IR, remember that you have a calculator. Once you've plotted out your numbers, call up the on-screen calculator and use it.

2

- Create variables as needed, and remember algebra traps:
  - For instance, on a two-part problem, you might need to solve for a "combo" of two variables, rather than for each variable separately.

- Consider alternatives to algebra:
  - For instance, plug real numbers or work backwards from the answer choices.

- As you test cases on a "true/false" question, play devil's advocate.
  - Once you have an example going one way, look for counterexamples going the other way.
  - You often do the same thing on Data Sufficiency.

- As an alternative to brute force, look for shortcuts:
  - For instance, rather than count lots of cases that fit some criteria, count the cases that *don't* fit and subtract from the total. This "$1 - x$" trick is useful on GMAT Quant as well.

4. Solve the Problem

Now execute your plan of attack. If you've done the first three steps right, solving should be pretty straightforward. Of course, you still need to take care. Write things down clearly, so that you don't make silly mistakes. Once you have figured out what the question really wants, the task is sometimes super-easy: *count the dots in this quadrant!* But you'd hate to mess up at this point. For instance, do algebraic manipulations on paper, and don't skip steps.

Here are a couple of tips specific to IR:

- When you extract numbers from a graph, write them down with labels. If you are pulling a point from a scatterplot, use (x, y) notation. Don't reverse x and y! If you have to estimate, do your best in the moment and keep going.

- To count entries in a sortable table, re-sort the table so that you group together the right entries. Then point at the screen and count under your breath. Who cares whether anyone's looking! To be even more secure, make hashmarks (卌 ||) or even jot labels on your paper.

- Write down any computations *before* you plug into your calculator. You might see a way to simplify first. For example, you can take 23% off $87.50 in two ways:
  - (a) $87.50 - (0.23)(87.50) = ?$
  - (b) $(0.77)(87.50) = ?$
    - Plan (b) is a little easier, faster, and less prone to error.

If you get stuck, quickly scan your work to see whether you made a simple mistake. Then back up and try another approach. Don't over-force your original method.

Example Problems

1. Two water storage tanks, Tank A and Tank B, can each hold more than 20,000 liters of water. Currently, Tank A contains 5,000 liters of water, while Tank B contains 8,000 liters. Each tank is being filled at a constant rate, such that in 15 hours, the two tanks will contain the same amount of water, though neither will be full.

In the table below, identify rates of filling for each tank that are together consistent with the information. Make only one selection in each column.

Tank A Fill Rate	Tank B Fill Rate	
○	○	30 liters/hr
○	◉	90 liters/hr
○	○	150 liters/hr
○	○	220 liters/hr
◉	○	290 liters/hr

Stop! Take your time to understand the prompt and to understand the question fully. Those are the first two steps of the problem-solving process

Okay, now what? What approach should you take?

Fortunately, the answer table gives you a hint—they want the fill rates of the tanks. So why not create variables for those rates?

We'll model the thinking process you might go through. You are the little person on the left.

"Ok, so let's say the filling rate of tank A is a, and the filling rate of Tank B is b. The rates are in liters per hour. So in 15 hours, Tank A has the original 5,000 liters, plus 15 hours of filling, or 15 hours times a liters per hour."

Tank A: $5,000 + 15a$

"Meanwhile, at the 15-hour mark, Tank B has its original 8,000 liters, plus 15 hours times b liters per hour."

Tank B: $8,000 + 15b$

"I can set those amounts equal, because the tanks have the *same* amount of water at that point in time."

$5,000 + 15a = 8,000 + 15b$

2

"Uh-oh. There is only one equation and there are two variables! Hmm. The question asks for choices that are 'consistent' with this information, meaning that there is more than one possible answer for each variable. Let's keep going. I can rearrange the equation, putting variables on one side and numbers on the other."

$$15a - 15b = 8,000 - 5,000 = 3,000$$

"Ahh! This is like a combo question! The key is to solve for $a - b$."

$$15(a - b) = 3,000$$
$$a - b = 3,000/15 = 200$$

"So now just find options in the table that differ by 200. The only ones that work are 290 and 90. So a must be 290, and b must be 90."

Your answers should look like this:

Tank A Fill Rate	Tank B Fill Rate	
○	○	30 liters/hr
○	◉	90 liters/hr
○	○	150 liters/hr
○	○	220 liters/hr
◉	○	290 liters/hr

Don't reverse the dots in the columns! You'll get the problem 100% wrong.

This problem probably feels like one you could encounter in the regular GMAT Quant section, except for the funny answer-choice format. That's right—some IR problems are essentially GMAT Quant problems in an IR costume.

By the way, never try to backsolve a two-part problem by testing every possible combination of numbers in the answer choices. There are too many possibilities. Instead, look for an algebraic approach or another shortcut.

Here's another example.

> 2. A juice bottling plant has purchased a new electric bottling machine. Working at a constant rate, the machine bottles R liters of juice per hour. As the machine works, it bottles C liters of juice per dollar spent on its operating and maintenance costs.
>
> In terms of R and C, determine how many hours it will take to spend $20 on the machine's operating and maintenance costs. Then determine how many dollars will be spent in 3 minutes. Make one choice in each column.

Hours to Spend $20	Dollars Spent in 3 Minutes	
○	○	$\dfrac{20}{RC}$
○	○	$\dfrac{20R}{C}$
◉	○	$\dfrac{20C}{R}$
○	○	$\dfrac{R}{20C}$
○	○	$\dfrac{RC}{20}$
○	○	$\dfrac{C}{20R}$

(handwritten notes in margin:)

1 L   per 30 mins

$\dfrac{C}{\text{litres of juice}}$ $\dfrac{1/R}{\text{litres juice}}$
dollar spent hour

$20 \dfrac{C}{R}$

$1/C \times 1/R$

Again, what do you do first? Read and really understand the prompt and the question! (A little time elapses, while you go back and make sure.)

Now let's focus on the first column. One approach is to use units to set up the algebra. You could work backwards from what you're looking for: hours.

"Okay, I need hours in my answer, and I've got $20 to spend. The more dollars, the more hours it'll take to spend them. This is kind of a rate problem, so if I set up dollars times hours per dollar, then I get hours."

$$\text{dollars} \times \frac{\text{hours}}{\text{dollar}} = \text{hours}$$

$$\$20 \times \frac{\text{hours}}{\$} = \text{hours}$$

2

"All right, what units do I have with the variables? R is liters per hour, and C is liters per dollar. Let's write these out."

$$R = \frac{\text{liters}}{\text{hour}} \qquad C = \frac{\text{liters}}{\$}$$

"How do I get hours per dollar? Somehow I have to divide one by the other, to get liters to cancel. If I put C on top, then dollars go in the denominator. Looks right."

$$\frac{C}{R} = \frac{\dfrac{\text{liters}}{\$}}{\dfrac{\text{liters}}{\text{hour}}} = \frac{\text{liters}}{\$} \times \frac{\text{hours}}{\text{liter}} = \frac{\cancel{\text{liters}}}{\$} \times \frac{\text{hours}}{\cancel{\text{liter}}} = \frac{\text{hours}}{\$}$$

"So the answer must be 20 times C over R."

$$\$20 \times \frac{\text{hours}}{\$} = 20 \times \frac{C}{R} = \frac{20C}{R} = \text{hours}$$

The correct answer for the first column is the third choice:

Hours to Spend $20	Dollars Spent in 3 Minutes	
○	○	$\dfrac{20}{RC}$
○	○	$\dfrac{20R}{C}$
◉	○	$\dfrac{20C}{R}$
○	○	$\dfrac{R}{20C}$
○	○	$\dfrac{RC}{20}$
○	○	$\dfrac{C}{20R}$

Alternatively, you could plug in numbers and test the answer choices.

"Okay, say the machine makes 10 liters of juice per hour, and it can bottle 2 liters for every dollar we spend on operating costs. So that means for the 10 liters we make in an hour, we spend $5. So we're spending $5 per hour."

$R = 10$ liters per hour
$C = 2$ liters per dollar
spend $5 per hour

"How long will it take us to spend $20? Divide $20 by $5 per hour, to get 4 hours."

$20 ÷ $5/hr = 4 hrs

"Now let's test the answer choices. Plug in 10 for R and 2 for C, and see which one equals 4. Only $\dfrac{20C}{R}$ works."

Which method is better? It just depends on what you see first and what is easiest for you. Don't force yourself to solve in some particular way because it is the "right" way. Let yourself be creative about how to solve.

Go back and solve the second part of the problem, confirming that that answer is $\dfrac{R}{20C}$. Note that 3 minutes $= \dfrac{1}{20}$ of an hour.

Before we look at the next example problem, recall that Either/Or Statements (which you encounter on Table Analysis and Multi-Source Reasoning problems) ask you to pick a side for each statement: yes or no, true or false, provable or unprovable, etc. With such problems, play devil's advocate. If you think the statement is likely to be true, look for a way in which the statement could be false. Whether you succeed in finding such a way or not, you'll have a much more grounded opinion about the statement.

2

3. The table below displays data from the different divisions of Company X in 2011. Market shares are computed by dividing Company X's total sales (in dollars) for that division by the total sales (in dollars) made by all companies selling products in that category. Market shares are separately calculated for the world (global market share) and for the United States (U.S. market share). Ranks are calculated relative to all companies competing in a particular market.

Division	Global Market Share	Global Market Rank	Total U.S. Market Share	U.S. Market Rank
Agriculture & Food	8%	6	12%	4
Healthcare & Medical	12%	4	18%	2
Household Goods & Personal Care	5%	5	10%	4
Performance Plastics	30%	1	26%	1
Water & Process Solutions	19%	1	32%	1

Select *Yes* if the statement can be proven true by the evidence provided. Otherwise, select *No*.

Yes	No	
O	O	There is at least one other country in which Company X has a greater percentage of the performance plastics market, as a percentage of 2011 sales, than it has of the performance plastics market in the U.S.

What's first? (1) Understand the prompt, and (2) understand the question. Take real time to do so here, since you have complex data and a statement that is worded in a cumbersome way.

Now, as you consider your approach, it may seem as if the answer to this question is *No*. How can you prove such a statement? All we know about performance plastics is that Company X has 26% of the U.S. market and 30% of the world market, and that both positions are #1 (meaning that no other company has a larger share of either market).

Well, let's play "devil's advocate" and try to poke a hole in the statement.

Imagine that the statement is false. That is, there is *no* other country in which X's share is greater than it is in the U.S. So in every other country, X's share of the market is 26% or less. Everywhere in the world, including in the U.S., Company X is making only 26% or less of the revenues that are being made on performance plastics.

Then how can X's share of the *world* market be 30%?

It can't be!

If Company X's global market share is 30%, but its market share in the U.S. is *lower* than 30%, then somewhere else, its market share must be *higher* than 30%. You can think of weighted averages. Company X's global market share is the weighted average of its market shares in all countries. For 30% to be the weighted average of 26% and a bunch of other numbers, at least one of those other numbers must be greater than 30%.

Thus, the statement must be true. The answer is *Yes*.

Here's the last example in this section:

4. Consider the graph below:

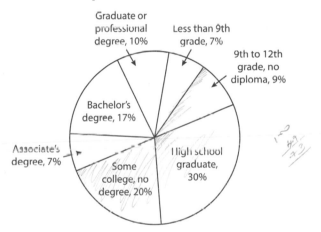

The percent of the population aged 25 Years and over that did NOT have a

bachelor's, graduate, or professional degree is ⬚Select... ⬚ .

7%
16%
27%
59%
73%

As always, carefully read the prompt and the question. Recognize that you are looking for a group for which something is NOT true.

Now, you could add the percentages of all of the groups that do *not* have a bachelor's, graduate, or professional degree. But that path is more time-consuming. Instead, add the two groups of people who actually have one of these degrees, and then subtract the result from 100%.

2

17% (bachelor's) + 10% (graduate or professional) = 27%

So 100% − 27% = 73% do NOT have one of these degrees.

Pick the last choice in the drop-down menu:

Select... ▼
7%
16%
27%
59%
73%

This "1 − x" technique is helpful for fraction, percentage, and even probability problems. Don't forget to subtract 27% from 100%! Be careful, because 27% is itself an answer choice.

Again, this problem could easily be on the regular GMAT Quant section. All that makes it IR-like is the drop-down menu.

Quant Topics Emphasized

Technically, any part of GMAT math is fair game on Integrated Reasoning. But two areas are worth calling out:

1.   Decimals, Percents, & Ratios
2.   Statistics

Let's take these in turn.

Decimals, Percents, & Ratios

For the GMAT as a whole, you need Fractions, Decimals, & Percents (FDPs). You need them on IR too, but with less emphasis on fractions; meanwhile, ratios step in. Here are the key differences in how the GMAT sections treat this topic:

Integrated Reasoning – *Real World*	GMAT Quant – *Math Tricks*
Decimals and percents are encountered more often than fractions. **Ratios** are also important.	Fractions are used extensively. Fraction math skills are very important.
Example: Which of the following stocks has the highest price-to-earnings ratio?	*Example:* $\dfrac{1}{3x} + \dfrac{3}{4 + \dfrac{2}{x}} = ?$

Percent problems draw on "real" data in graph, chart, and paragraph form.	Percent problems can be more abstract or contrived.
Example: Was the percent increase in imports from China to the U.S. greater than the percent increase in imports from Brazil to the U.S.?	*Example:* If *x* is *y*% of *z*, what is *y*% of *x* in terms of *z*?

For both IR and regular GMAT Quant, you need to know standard percent formulas, such as the percent change formula $\frac{\text{New} - \text{Old}}{\text{Old}} = 100\%$. On IR, you get one bonus tool: the online calculator, which even has a $\boxed{\%}$ button. This can save you time and mental energy. For instance, to increase 107.5 by 17%, you can either multiply 107.5 by 1.17 or add 17% to 107.5, using the $\boxed{\%}$ key:

(a) $\boxed{1}\,\boxed{0}\,\boxed{7}\,\boxed{.}\,\boxed{5}\quad\boxed{*}\quad\boxed{1}\,\boxed{.}\,\boxed{1}\,\boxed{7}\quad\boxed{=}$

(b) $\boxed{1}\,\boxed{0}\,\boxed{7}\,\boxed{.}\,\boxed{5}\quad\boxed{+}\quad\boxed{1}\,\boxed{7}\,\boxed{\%}\quad\boxed{=}$

Either way gets you 125.775.

Is 105.5 + 19% larger? Don't look for an estimation shortcut. Just punch it in and see. (It's not — the result is 125.545.)

If you are not already very comfortable with solving percent and decimal problems, review core GMAT Quant materials, such as the Manhattan GMAT *Fractions, Decimals, & Percents Strategy Guide.* The rest of this section describes only the new wrinkles that IR adds to these sorts of problems.

Common Percent Question Traps

Several common traps show up regularly in percent problems. Forewarned is forearmed. Here are four "percent traps" that you are likely to see on the IR section:

1. **Percents vs. Quantities.** Some numbers in FDP problems are percents. Others are quantities. Don't mistake one for the other, especially when numbers are embedded in text:

    If a carrot has a higher percentage of vitamin A relative to its total vitamin composition than a mango does, does the carrot have more vitamin A than the mango does?

    The answer is that you don't know, because you don't know the total vitamin content of either the carrot or the mango. *Perhaps carrots have a lot less vitamin content overall than mangos.* A big fraction of a small whole could certainly be less (in grams, say) than a smaller fraction of a bigger whole.

2

2. **Percent Of What.** Don't assume that all of the percents given are percents of the total. Some of the percents given may well be percents of something *other* than the grand total. If you miss that little detail, you will get the answer wrong.

    If 60% of customers at the produce stand purchased fruit and 20% of fruit purchasers purchased bananas, what percent of customers did not purchase bananas?

    A casual reader might see "20%… purchased bananas" and immediately decide that the answer must be 80%. However, the problem says that 20% *of fruit purchasers* purchased bananas. Fruit purchasers are a *subset* of the total—only 60%. So the banana-buying percent of *all* customers is just $0.60 \times 0.20 = 0.12$, or 12%. The answer is $100\% - 12\% = 88\%$, not 80%.

    Slow down when you read problems such as this one. Confirm what exactly you're taking a percent of.

3. **Percent *Of* vs. Percent *Greater Than*.** Look carefully at the following two questions:

    1. 10 is what percent of 8?
    2. 10 is what percent greater than 8?

    The first question just asks for a simple percent *of.* The answer is 10/8, or 125%.

    The second question asks for a percent *change* or percent *comparison*. The answer is $(10 - 8)/8$, or 25%.

    The wording looks similar. As always, slow down and read carefully. Pay attention to the little words *after* the word "percent" or the symbol %.

4. **Percent Decrease and Then Increase.**

    If the price of lettuce is decreased by 20% and then the decreased price is later increased by 22%, is the resulting final price less than, equal to, or greater than the original price?

    The resulting price is less than the original price, *not* equal to it or greater than it. In fact, if you decrease the price by 20%, you would have to increase the decreased price by 25% to get back to the original price.

    Plug in a number to see it for yourself. $100 is nice. If you decrease $100 by 20%, you get $80.

2

You would have to increase $80 by 25% to get back to $100. (25% of $80 is the $20 increase you need.) Increasing $80 by 22% yields $97.60, which is less than $100.

Statistics

Statistics is important on Integrated Reasoning, because this section is about real-world data, and statistics give you a handle on data. In contrast, statistics on GMAT Quant provide just another way to ask a clever math question.

Integrated Reasoning – *Real World*	GMAT Quant – *Math Tricks*
Real-world statistical terms, including regression and correlation, are used to describe realistic data presented in tables and charts. *Example:* The mean age of the participants in the marketing study is 24.	Statistics terms, such as mean and median, are used primarily to create tricky problems based on contrived data, such as sets of consecutive integers. *Example:* How much greater than the mean is the median of the set of integers n, $n + 2$, $n + 4$, and $n + 6$?
Coordinate plane axes (x and y) may not work like functions. On a scatterplot, a single x value may be associated with more than one y value.	Scatterplots are absent. In the coordinate plane, y is typically a function of x.

When you have a lot of quantitative information, statistics can help boil it down to a few key numbers so that you can make good probabilistic predictions and better decisions. The word **statistics** can refer either to the subject ("Stats make sense to me now that I've learned what they mean") or to the key numbers themselves ("Wow! These performance statistics are so good that they look rigged").

This section covers every statistics concept you need for IR. Most of the statistics questions on the IR section just require that you understand certain definitions, but in business school, you will take at least one statistics course and will have to perform plenty of statistical analyses. The "leg up" you get now on stats for the GMAT will help you in b-school. See our book *Case Studies & Cocktails*, from which this presentation borrows liberally.

Descriptive Statistics

Say there are 500 people in your business school class and you want to think about the *number of years* each of you spent working between college graduation and business school.

To make things simple, you'll probably round to the nearest whole number (instead of having data like 5.25 years, 7.8 years, etc.). Whole numbers are *discrete* (meaning "separated and countable"), so with this information, you can make a *histogram* to display the count in each category.

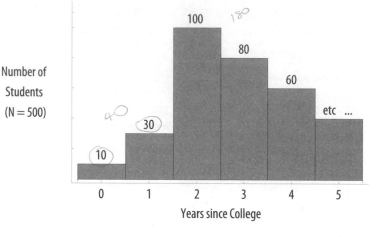

If you convert to percents, you can show the same graph as a **frequency distribution**.

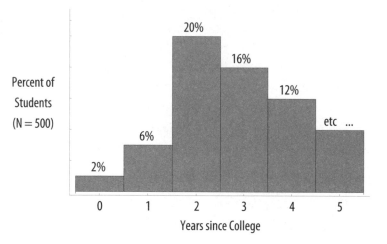

This pretty picture illustrates a link between statistics and *probability*. If you pick someone at random from your class, there's a 2% chance he or she spent 0 years working, a 6% chance he or she spent 1 year working, etc.

Now, what's the **average** amount of time your classmates have spent in the real world since college? There are three primary ways to answer this question:

1. Mean
2. Median   } Three types of average
3. Mode

The mean is the most important. In fact, this is what Excel (everyone's favorite spreadsheet program) calls AVERAGE. Technically, this is the "arithmetic mean" (air-ith-MET-ik), but the GMAT never uses the other means defined by statisticians, so we can just say "mean." You already know the formula from the GMAT Quant section:

$$\text{Mean} = \frac{\text{Sum of all years}}{\text{Number of numbers}}$$

You add up everyone's "years since college" and divide that total by 500, the number of people in your class:

$$\text{Mean Years} = \frac{\text{Total years}}{\text{Number of students}}$$

$$3.36 = \frac{1,680}{500}$$

You could just add up each person's number of years since college to get the Total Years, but there is a faster way. Since a lot of the numbers are repeated, it makes sense to add them in groups:

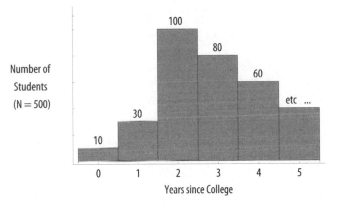

Ten 0's is ten times zero. Rewriting, you get:

$$\text{Mean} = \frac{10\times0 + 30\times1 + 100\times2 + 80\times3 + \ldots}{500}$$

Now split up the numerator:

$$\text{Mean} = \frac{10}{500}\times0 + \frac{30}{500}\times1 + \frac{100}{500}\times2 + \frac{80}{500}\times3 + \ldots$$

$$= 2\%\times0 + 6\%\times1 + 20\%\times2 + 16\%\times3 + \ldots$$

Notice that the percents you just calculated are the same as those on the frequency distribution:

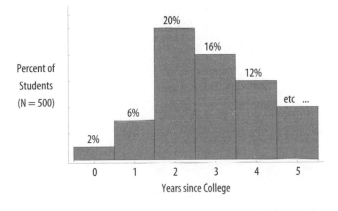

If the frequencies are percents or decimals, you can find the mean by multiplying each observation by its frequency and adding up the results. This is the same technique used to compute a weighted average. The mean really is the "average" value, computed by weighting each observed value by its frequency. The mean is also sometimes referred to as the **expected value** of x. It's the "average" value you'd expect if you pulled a lot of people at random and averaged their x's (years since college).

The **median** is the middle number, or the 50th percentile: half of the people have more years since college (or the same number), and half have fewer years (or the same number). You can read the median from the percent histogram—just add from the left until you hit at least 50%. The median of the Years since College distribution is 4 years.

The **mode** is the observation that shows up the most often, corresponding to the highest frequency on the histogram. If none of the years to the right of 4 have more than 20% of the population, then the histogram's peak is 20% and the mode is 2 years.

The Spread

Mean, median, and mode are all "central" measures—they answer the question "where's the center of all the data?" But often, you need to know how spread out the data is.

The crudest measure of spread is **range**, which is just the largest value minus the smallest value. While range is easy to calculate, it's susceptible to **outliers**—oddball observations that, rightly or wrongly, lie far away from most of the others. For example, if one person in your program is in her 70s and has been out of school for 50 years, then your range of Years since College would be huge because of that one outlier. Outliers are sometimes erroneous data (someone types in 55 instead of 5) but not always.

A better measure of spread is **standard deviation**. You will never have to calculate standard deviation on the GMAT because it is such a pain to do so without Excel or other software, but you should know how it is calculated. So here's how it's done:

1. Figure out the mean.
2. Subtract the mean value from the value of each observation and square those differences, also known as **deviations**.
3. Take the mean of all of those squared deviations. This result is known as the **variance**.
4. Finally, take the square root of the variance. That's the standard deviation.

Roughly, standard deviation indicates how far on average a data point is from the mean, whether above or below (which would be average distance). That's not the precise mathematical definition, but it's close enough for the GMAT.

Consider a few distributions of data with the same mean of 4, but different spreads:

Case 1: Every observation = 4

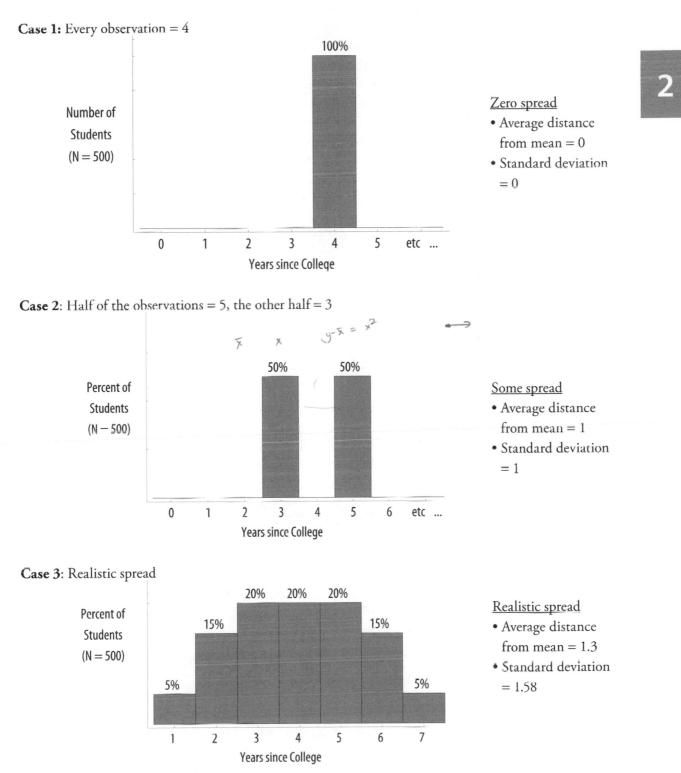

Zero spread
- Average distance from mean = 0
- Standard deviation = 0

Case 2: Half of the observations = 5, the other half = 3

Some spread
- Average distance from mean = 1
- Standard deviation = 1

Case 3: Realistic spread

Realistic spread
- Average distance from mean = 1.3
- Standard deviation = 1.58

In the last case, the average distance from 4 and the standard deviation (defined by the weird procedure earlier) are not exactly the same, but they are pretty close. By the way, these numbers are not "4 plus or minus 1.58." Often, there's a significant amount of data *more* than a standard deviation away from the

mean. But when the histogram is bell-shaped (with one central bump and two little *tails* like a bell seen from the side), more than half of the data is within 1 standard deviation of the mean.

Standard deviation is incredibly important in finance, operations, and other subjects. For now, focus on an intuitive understanding. For instance, if you add outliers, the standard deviation increases. If you remove outliers, it decreases. If you just shift every number up by 1, the standard deviation stays the same.

The Normal Distribution

The most important distribution in statistics is the **normal distribution**, also known as the bell curve.

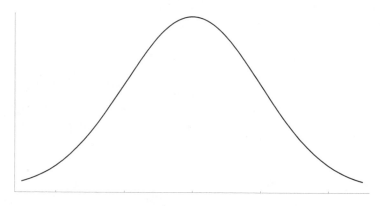

Every normal distribution has essentially the same shape: a central hump with two long, symmetrical tails on either side. The peak of the hump is centered over the mean. So if some population of people has a mean weight of 150 pounds, and that weight is "normally distributed," then the distribution looks like this:

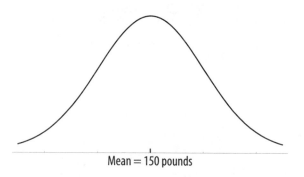

Mean = 150 pounds

The other thing that you have to specify about the normal distribution is how spread out it is:

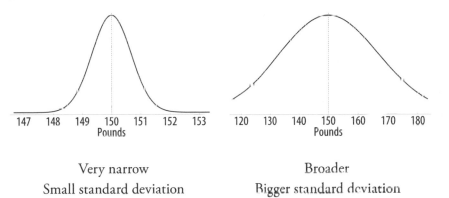

Very narrow	Broader
Small standard deviation	Bigger standard deviation

The standard deviation provides a great yardstick for these normal curves. About a third of the data will lie within 1 standard deviation above the mean, and another third will lie within 1 standard below it. About 95% of the data will lie within 2 standard deviations of the mean. If you know the mean and you know the standard deviation, you know everything you need to know about normally distributed data.

Correlation

Up to now, everything has had to do with one variable—one measurement:

Student	Years since College
You	4
Alice Atwater	2
Bill Burns	6
...	...

One variable for each observation.

What if you get *two* pieces of data about each person? Now you can look at more interesting patterns:

Student	Years since College	Height
You	4	5 feet 7 inches
Alice Atwater	2	5 feet 10 inches
Bill Burns	6	5 feet 2 inches
...	...	...

2

To look for a pattern, you put all of these observations on a scatterplot:

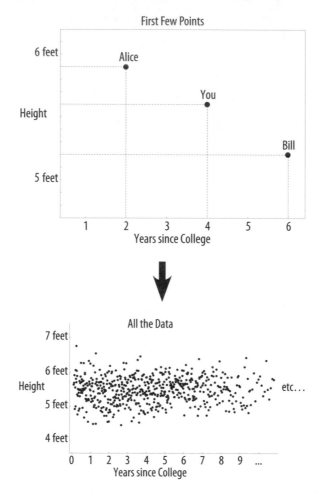

The second graph would almost certainly reveal no overall pattern. The " shotgun blast" shows that two variables, Years since College and Height, are basically **uncorrelated**. There is **no relationship**.

In contrast, if you plot Years since College versus Age, you'll get a pattern. Typically, older people have been out of college longer — no surprise.

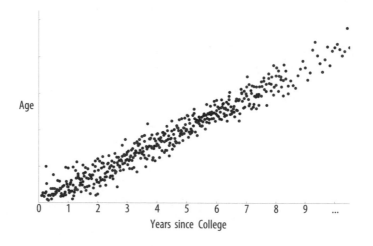

Most people are either high on both scales or low on both scales. This means that Years since College and Age are highly **correlated**. There is a **positive relationship** between the two variables.

You can measure the degree of correlation with *r*, the **correlation coefficient**. You will never be asked to calculate *r* on the GMAT. The important thing is to understand what the *correlation coefficient* tells you.

Range of *r*	Correlation	Pattern	
1 (max)	Perfect positive	All points lie on a line of positive slope	
0.*something*	Positive	Points cluster around a line of positive slope	
0	None	No pattern (shotgun blast) *or* a non-linear pattern	
−0.*something*	Negative	Points cluster around a line of negative slope	
−1 (min)	Perfect negative	All points lie on a line of negative slope	

Notice that *r doesn't* tell you the slope of the line. What *r* tells you is the sign of that slope, and more importantly, how tightly the points cluster around a line of positive or negative slope.

Regression

"Doing a linear regression" means finding the **best-fit line** through a scatterplot. With such a line you can describe the relationship between *x* and *y* more precisely and even predict values of *y* from values of *x*:

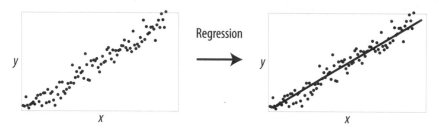

The best-fit regression line minimizes the distance, in some sense, between the points and the line. You can see this intuitively:

Terrible fit   Better fit   Best fit

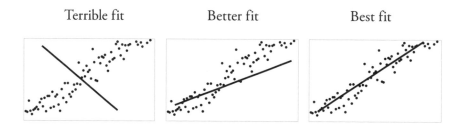

The GMAT will never ask you compute a linear regression, but a graphical IR question might ask about the slope of a regression line:

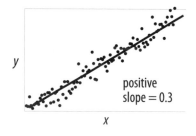

positive
slope = 0.3

"If *x* increases by 1, *y* goes up
by 0.3 on average."

If the two variables are positively correlated, then the regression line will have positive slope, demonstrating a positive relationship. Likewise, negative correlation = negative slope of regression line = negative relationship.

Remember that to find a line is to find its equation. The general equation of a line is $y = mx + b$, as you know from your GMAT Geometry preparation. The letter m represents the **slope** of the line, while b represents the **y-intercept**, where the line crosses the y-axis:

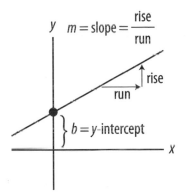

A line with equation $y = 3x - 2$ intercepts the y-axis at $(0, -2)$. On this line, if x increases by 1, y increases by 3:

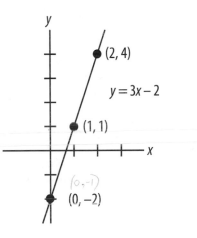

Finding the line means finding the values for the slope m and the y-intercept b.

Types of Tables and Graphs

The Integrated Reasoning section displays data in all kinds of ways. Here's a glimpse of many of the beasts in the "graph zoo":

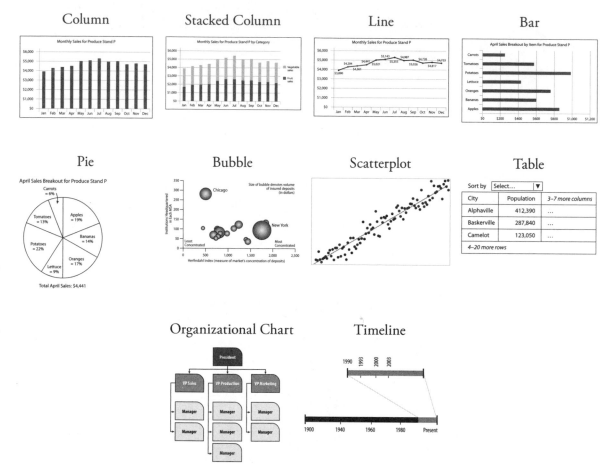

Don't let all these columns, lines, and bubbles raise your blood pressure. These display formats are commonly used in business and academic settings today—and you've seen most, if not all, of these animals before. The GMAT will only rarely force you to figure out some really weird chart or graph. ("Chart" and "graph" are interchangeable words in this context.)

Static Tables

A static table (one you can't re-sort) presents data in simple rows and columns. When you run into a static table, figure out what kind of information is in each row and column. Consider this table:

Monthly Sales Breakout for Produce Stand P

Month	Total ($)	% Fruit	% Vegetable
Jan	3,890	44.29	55.71
Feb	4,204	45.74	54.26
Mar	4,361	45.10	54.90
Apr	4,441	45.94	54.06
May	5,021	49.17	50.83
Jun	5,143	52.40	47.60
Jul	5,355	50.38	49.62
Aug	4,987	51.41	48.59
Sep	5,026	51.21	48.79
Oct	4,726	49.89	50.11
Nov	4,817	49.78	50.22
Dec	4,723	47.77	52.23

Don't skip the title! What's in this table? The monthly sales for some produce stand. Each row represents a different month. The columns represent the information available for each month, namely the $ sales and the proportion of those sales that were fruits or vegetables.

You can generally think of each row as a record. For instance, the first row is the record for the month of January. Each column corresponds to a field, or a bit of information, in that record.

Often, tables contain a mix of absolute quantities and percents. Be careful not to confuse the two. Individual percents are not always labeled with a percent sign, but percent *rows* or *columns* are labeled as such. That's another reason to pay close attention to the labels.

If you are given a static table, you will be able to complete the task in a reasonable amount of time *without* having to sort the table. For instance, you might just have to look a piece of information up. The hard part will come next (what you should *do* with the information you just looked up). For example:

> Were the dollar sales of fruit higher in July or August?

Go get the total sales and the % fruit for each month. Multiply them together on the calculator:

July fruit sales = 50.38% of $5,355 = 0.5038 × $5,355 = $2,697.85
August fruit sales = 51.41% of $4,987 = 0.5141 × $4,987 = $2,563.82

So fruit sales were slightly higher in July.

Sortable Tables

A sortable table (in Table Analysis) is likely to be bigger than a static table, but not always. For instance, this table contains fewer numbers than the previous one.

Sort by: [Select... ▼]

Item	Annual Revenue Contribution	Revenue Ranking	Annual Profit Margin %	Profitability Ranking
Bananas	$3,421	3	11.9%	2
Cantaloupe	$1,945	14	10.5%	5
Grapes	$3,835	1	12.2%	1
Lettuce	$2,966	5	11.1%	3
Tomatoes	$3,152	4	10.7%	4
Potatoes	$2,578	10	9.9%	15
Zucchini	$984	27	10.4%	6

You should approach a sortable table the same way as you do a static table — figure out the contents using the title, row labels, and column labels. Next, play around with the sorting function, which is not a gimmick. It's theoretically possible to solve a problem with a sortable table without re-sorting, but it will be much easier if you do re-sort. You will always be asked three Either/Or Statements about a sortable table. To make your call on each statement, you will probably want to sort by a different column.

By the way, if you have Excel experience, there is no "secondary sort" on IR. You can only sort by one column at a time. Re-sorting erases the effects of any previous sort.

Some tables contain ranks (#1, #2, etc.) in one column that may seem redundant with another column. You may wonder why GMAT gives you ranks instead of just letting you sort and figure it out for yourself. That's a good thing to wonder, because the presence of ranks means that you will have to infer something from the rank that isn't shown. Perhaps not all items included in the *ranking* are included in the *table*. Look above: what item ranks second in annual revenue contribution? You don't know! There's no 2 in the Revenue Ranking column. You do know that #1 is #1, though, so no other item (including those not shown) ranked higher than grapes in either revenue or profitability.

Column and Bar Charts

A column chart shows amounts as heights, highlighting changes in those heights as you read from left to right. Similarly, bar charts show amounts as lengths, highlighting differences in those lengths as you scan from top to bottom.

Column

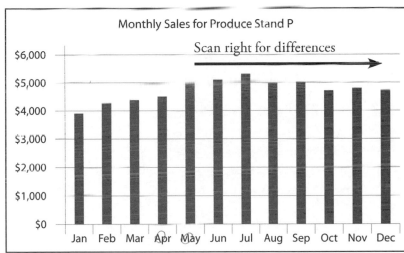

Monthly Sales for Produce Stand P

Scan right for differences

Bar

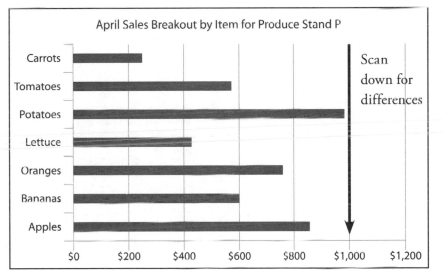

April Sales Breakout by Item for Produce Stand P

Scan down for differences

Column charts can be used to show trends over time, while bar charts are more frequently used for non-time comparisons (e.g., carrots vs. apples).

The hardest thing about a column or bar chart might just be reading a value from a column or bar that ends *between* gridlines. The GMAT will never make an exact value critical if you have to estimate, so just use your finger or a piece of paper to make a straight line and take your best guess.

With a column chart, you might need to calculate the percent increase or decrease from one time period to the next. Consider the monthly sales chart above, and answer the following:

What was the approximate percent increase in sales from April to May?

2

Estimate April sales to be $4,500 (the column ends about halfway between $4,000 and $5,000). May's column ends right on $5,000. Now use the percent change formula:

$$\frac{\text{May sales} - \text{April sales}}{\text{April sales}} \approx \frac{5,000 - 4,500}{4,500} = \frac{1}{9} \approx 11\%$$

Variations on Column and Bar Charts

If there is more than one series of numbers, the GMAT might use a stacked or clustered column chart. The stacked form emphasizes the sum of the two series of numbers, while the clustered form highlights which one is bigger at any point along the way.

Stacked Column — *Emphasizes Sums*

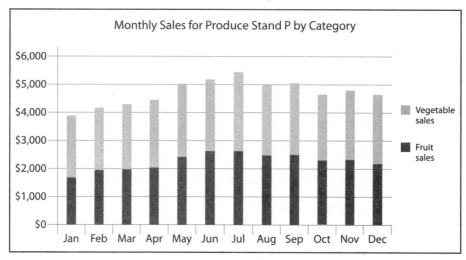

Clustered Column — *Emphasizes Differences*

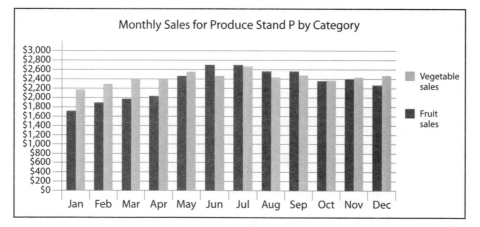

In the stacked column, it is hard to read off "Vegetable Sales" by itself—you have to subtract "Total Sales" minus "Fruit Sales." So, of course, be ready to answer a question of this nature. Similarly, if you

2

have a clustered form, you may have to compute the total on your own. The IR question writers will sometimes make you work against the grain.

Line Charts

Line charts are very similar to column charts. However, each number is shown as a floating dot rather than as a column, and the dots are connected by lines. The x-axis almost always represents time, since the lines imply connection. Although lines are continuous, do *not* assume that the data is itself continuous. If it is monthly data, it is monthly data—the line doesn't show you day-by-day. Multiple lines show multiple data series changing over time more clearly than clustered columns do.

Line

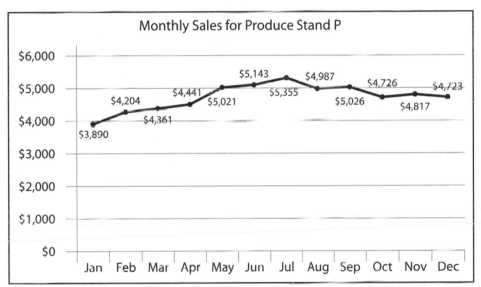

Line (with 2 data series)

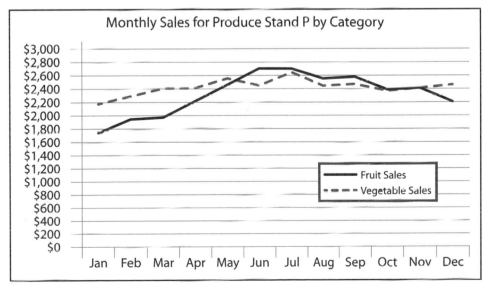

Pie Charts

A pie chart is used to show the relative sizes of "slices" as proportions of a whole. The size of the angle of the pie slice is proportional to that item's percent of the whole. Even if a pie chart shows amounts instead of percent, data is only shown in pies when percents are important to the story. The GMAT would *not* use a pie chart if the pieces of the pie don't sum up to a meaningful whole. Percents on various slices will always be the same percent "of" (the whole).

Pie
April Sales Breakout for Produce Stand P

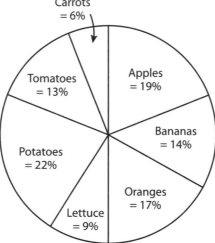

Total April Sales: $4,441

Since the total April sales figure is given, we can easily calculate the dollar sales of any item, or group of items, in the pie. That's a typical task with this type of chart.

You might be asked to calculate absolute quantities from the percents given on the pie chart:

> What is the total dollar value of lettuce and tomato sales for Produce stand P in April?

Lettuce & tomato sales = 9% + 13% = 22%. Remember, all these percents are of the same total ($4,441):

22% of $4,441 = 0.22 × $4,441 = $977.02

By the way, a pie chart can only show one series of data. If you see two pies, they represent two separate series of data.

MANHATTAN
GMAT

Scatterplots and Bubble Charts

A scatterplot is used to show the relationship between two columns of data in a table. Each point on the plot represents a single record (a single row). The overall pattern of the dots indicates how the two columns of numbers vary together, if at all:

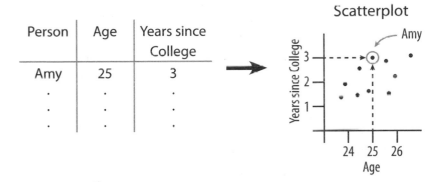

You might be asked whether the correlation between the two pieces of related data graphed is positive (slopes up) or negative (slopes down).

You might also see a **bubble chart**. A bubble chart looks intimidating, but it is just a scatterplot on steroids. Instead of two pieces of information about each point, you have *three*. In order to show that third dimension, all the little points get "pumped up" to various sizes, like Arnold Schwarzenegger's muscles—and those pumped-up sizes give you a relative measure of that third dimension. Look at the following real bubble chart:

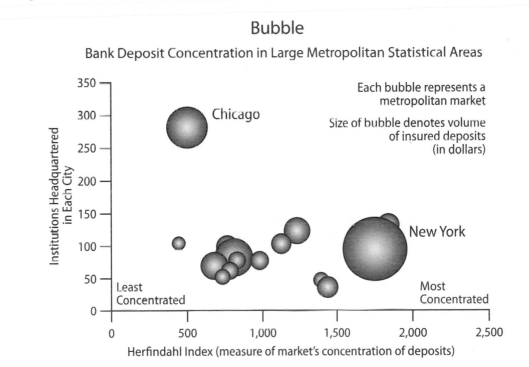

Sources: Summary of Deposits, June 2002; FDIC's Research and Information System, June 30, 2003.
Note: Fifteen largest markets shown, based on number of institutions headquartered there.

Although this graph looks very strange at first, it is well labeled. Compare Chicago and New York. You can see that New York has far fewer bank headquarters (y-axis value) than Chicago does, and that less money (size of the bubble, or z value) is deposited among more banks in Chicago than in New York. Finally, Chicago deposits are less "concentrated" (x-axis value) than New York deposits are.

Other Types of Charts

The graph zoo above is not exhaustive; you may encounter a rare bird or beast in your IR journey. Don't panic. Simply read the title, read the labels, and try to figure out how the graph is laid out visually. If you're stuck, focus on just one small part, such as a single point. What does that point represent? What do you know about that point? Then work your way out from there.

Although you may not be familiar with a new type of chart, you should be able to figure it out in 30 seconds or so. A GMAT chart is never pure chaos; it's always labeled and organized. The "org chart" and the expanded timeline shown below are good examples of unusual graphs that you can quickly decipher. Timelines don't have to run horizontally, by the way!

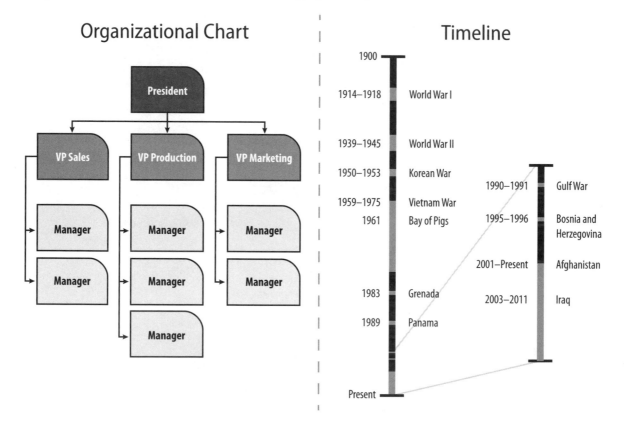

Typical org charts show hierarchical relationships within a business. Expanded timelines give you both a big picture of events in order and a "zoomed in" look at one part of the picture. Never forget that the scales in the different sections are different; be ready to make comparisons across those different scales.

Another type of slightly unusual chart that you might see is a Venn diagram:

Venn Diagram

Students Taking French, Spanish, Both or Neither

* Each square represents 5 students.

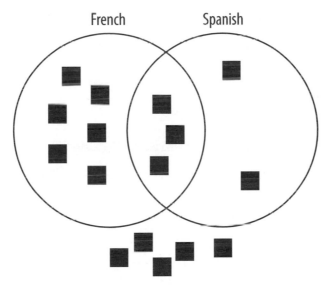

This type of chart displays membership in overlapping groups; it is more fully described in the Overlapping Sets chapter of the Manhattan GMAT *Word Problems Strategy Guide*. In the chart above, the two circles show the number of French and Spanish speakers. The overlapping region represents people who speak both of these languages, while the people who speak neither of the two languages are shown outside the circles. For example:

How many people in the school represented speak both French and Spanish?

There are 3 squares in the overlapping region, and each square represents 5 students. Thus:

3 squares × 5 students/square = 15 students.

When the Prompt Contains More Than One Graph or Chart

If there is more than one source of data, you are going to have to use them all. Fortunately, the different sources of data must be logically connected somehow. First, look for identical or similar labels. Be alert to slight differences. For instance, remember that $ sales of fruit in January are different from % sales of fruit in January. Also, what you are taking a percent *of* matters immensely.

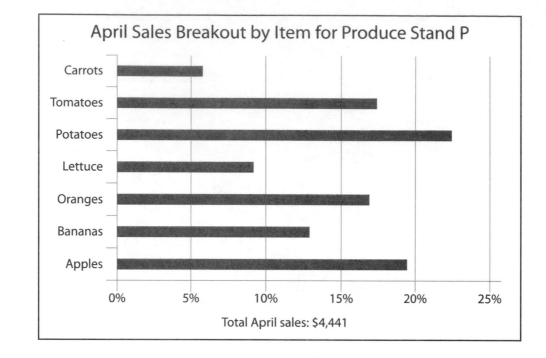

**Vitamin Content of Produce Items Sold
at Produce Stand P in April**

	Vitamin C Content	*Vitamin A Content*
Apples	low	low
Bananas	medium	low
Oranges	high	medium
Lettuce	high	low
Potatoes	medium	low
Tomatoes	high	high
Carrots	low	high

In the month of April, what were the total sales of produce items at Produce Stand P that were high in both vitamin A and vitamin C content?

You need to figure out *which* produce items were high in both vitamin A and vitamin C; then you can calculate the total sales of those items. The table shows you that only tomatoes are high in both vitamins A and C, so you just need total tomato sales.

The bar graph shows us that tomatoes account for about 17% of April sales and that total April sales were $4,441. So you need 17% of $4,441:

$$0.17 \times 4,441 = \$754.97$$

In Brief

To summarize this chapter:

Everything tested in the regular GMAT quant section is fair game in the Integrated Reasoning section. There is a new emphasis on graphs and real-world data, but the general problem-solving techniques that you have been practicing for GMAT Quant will still be effective on the IR section.

Stop yourself if you are trying to use math that isn't covered at all on the rest of the GMAT. The only real exception is computation—use the calculator for ugly numbers. You will never be asked anything that can't be solved quickly with a calculator and knowledge of standard GMAT math.

Take your time as you attack these problems. You will feel time pressure, but don't let it panic you. Follow a good process:

1.   Understand the prompt.
2.   Understand the question.
3.   Plan your approach.
4.   Solve the problem.

Pay attention to percents, decimals, and ratios, especially common percent traps. Also, review the statistics content in this chapter for general understanding. Finally, familiarize yourself with the most common denizens of the IR "graph zoo."

Chapter 3 of

Integrated Reasoning

IR Verbal

In This Chapter...

How to Tackle IR Verbal: Understand-Plan-Solve

"Critical Reading"

Playing Little Logic Games

Interpreting Real-World Communications

Chapter 3:

IR Verbal

Integrated Reasoning poses several challenges to the verbal side of your brain:

- You have a lot to read, just as on the GMAT Verbal section.
- Many prompts are fragmented, forcing you to connect the pieces.
- The text is wide-ranging in both content and form, even more than on GMAT Verbal.
- The text is integrated with numbers that you can't just gloss over.

Last but not least, you have to read *fast*. On the 30-minute IR section, you'll be battling the clock from start to finish.

Integrated Reasoning (30 minutes)	GMAT Verbal (75 minutes)
• Lots to read • Fragmented prompts • Wide-ranging content and form • Integrated with Quant	• Lots to read • Prompts in one piece • Somewhat narrower range of content and form • Not integrated with Quant

Tab #1   Tab #2   Tab #3

*Email from **manager** to staff*

The results of the recent marketing survey indicate that at least 73.1% of respondents have purchased Zirconium A in the past month, and 82.5% of respondents prefer Zirconium A. Therefore, we should be able to predict that…

Several models of supernova formation have been proposed since 1926, when the term "supernova" was apparently first used in print…
  Another paragraph about supernovas.
  Even more information about supernovas.

3

What does this mean? First of all, certain GMAT Verbal topics are unlikely to be tested. For instance, you don't have to worry about the formalities of grammar—those are covered by Sentence Correction. Likewise, you won't have to uncover hidden assumptions in an argument or analyze its structure, as you will on Critical Reasoning.

That said, you have to read grammatical sentences and understand their literal meaning. You also have to draw accurate logical inferences from textual evidence. In other words, you have to *apply* grammar and basic logic—just as you have to on Reading Comprehension, which is the GMAT Verbal question type most similar to what you face on IR.

With a RC passage, you have to find the right reading speed and mental distance. You can't just do a superficial skim, but you can't get lost in the details either. You'll have to strike a similar balance on IR.

Frequently, you'll have to draw non-trivial logical *inferences* from IR text. Think of the IR reading task as "Critical Reading":

Critical Reading = Reading Comprehension + a little Critical Reasoning
(+ even a little Data Sufficiency)

Some IR text that you'll need to process will be very much like an RC passage. At other times, you'll need to deal with brand-new sorts of prompts, as when you solve a small logical puzzle or interpret a dialogue. In all cases, though, you'll be asked to look up details and draw inferences.

How to Tackle IR Verbal: Understand-Plan-Solve

As with Integrated Reasoning Quant, you need a **good process** for IR Verbal. The process is ultimately the same as before:

1.   Understand the prompt.
2.   Understand the question.
3.   Plan your approach.
4.   Solve the problem.

Again, even if you find this aspect of IR straightforward, don't ignore process entirely. Experts can be victims of over-confidence. Following a good method can save your bacon.

1. Understand the Prompt

You have to be rigorous about getting the big picture quickly and effectively. Remember that some prompts—especially lengthy ones—will typically have more than one associated question, and those questions may have multiple parts. So it is worth investing time up front to grasp the prompt decently.

As you read over the different pieces of a verbal prompt, ask yourself **What** and **So What**, just as you do for a graph or table:

3

***What* is this?**

- What is in this tab, this row, or column? What do these points on the graph represent? What does this tab *tell* you?

- Simply saying to yourself "*This* is the kind of stuff I'm looking at" can help you keep the right mental distance from the material—you're close enough to know what it is, but not so close as to get lost in details.

So *What* about this?

- Why is this here? What purpose or role does it serve, relative to everything else? How does it fit in? Why is it important at all?

- Here, you are drawing connections between what you're looking at and what you've *already* looked at. At the start, simply look for the same labels, or similar ones. When you make a connection, pay extra attention to whatever's *different*. That contrast is often crucial.

- If the whole story makes sense, great, but if it's not 100% coherent, simply make the connections that you can and move on. There will always be corners that you have to leave unswept on the big-picture scan.

With the "What and So What" process, you can mentally organize a large mess of text, tables, and graphs in short order. What you're really doing is creating a **high-level mental map**. Use this process in business school when you first read a case.

Fragmentation of the IR prompt will actually help you with "What and So What," because things that look different or that are positioned differently are easier to keep straight in your memory. In ancient times, orators used this principle to remember speeches: what you do is associate various parts of the speech with different rooms in your house. Then you take a "memory walk" through the rooms to recall the speech. Oratory is not tested on the GMAT, of course, but you can solidify what and where things are by planting flags on your mental map as you go. You might even mutter to yourself:

"*First* tab… okay, in this email, the assistant is asking for an increase in the budget."
"*Second* tab… okay, the boss replies, she wants evidence that the current budget is too low."
"*Third* tab… facts from the assistant… arguing that expenses are growing along with headcount."

Just like a Reading Comprehension passage, a long IR prompt is always broken up into meaningful divisions. Make sense of that meaning by thinking about the relationships between the divisions.

If you really want to, take a few notes, as you might for an RC passage. Don't write a lot down, though; it'll take too long.

2. Understand the Question

When you read the question, read it carefully. What exactly does the GMAT want from you? Precise wording matters.

Also pay attention to the question format, particularly if it's unfamiliar. Traditional multiple-choice and pull-down statements are straightforward, but Either/Or statements and two-part questions can be tricky, because they look like each other. With Either/Or statements, you make a choice for every statement (every row has an answer). With two-part questions, you make only one choice in each column—many rows will have nothing filled in.

Some folks like to read the question first before grappling with the prompt. If so, be sure to come back to the specific wording of the question.

3. Plan Your Approach

Next, you have to figure out what to *do* with the prompt in order to answer the question:

- What do you have to go look up? What parts should you re-read?
- What pieces of information do you have to combine from different locations?
- What sorts of logical inferences do you have to draw?

You won't be able to determine every task before you start carrying them out. But before you rush back to the prompt and start a wild search, think about the *kinds* of information you're looking for. What would be sufficient to answer the question one way or another? This will guide your search.

4. Solve the Problem

Now go and execute the tasks you've set out for yourself. Unlike Quant, Verbal will only rarely require you to write things down as you solve. However, you should still be methodical. If you are following a lengthy chain of inferences, either notate your intermediate findings or mutter them under your breath.

As you walk through any chain of logic, challenge your thinking. Play a "devil's advocate" briefly but authentically. Does your inference *necessarily* follow? Are you making any unjustified assumptions? What if something in the background were somehow different?

You'll get a chance to try out this process shortly.

"Critical Reading"

Traditional multiple-choice questions on GMAT Verbal rarely have multiple parts—and when they do, the final choices are still (A) through (E), restricting the possible responses:

> Which of the following statements is supported by the passage?
> I. Some statement.
> II. Another statement.
> III. A third statement.
>
> (A) I only   (B) II only   (C) III only   (D) I and II only   (E) I, II, and III

In the example above, you simply can't answer "I and III only," even though that's logically possible. With the new Integrated Reasoning question formats, though, you answer each part independently. As a result, the GMAT can ask a series of Yes/No questions more cleanly, and such questions often have to do with logical inference:

- Is this statement supported by the information provided?
- Would this statement support the data provided in the table?
- Does this finding confirm the theory put forth by Fischer?
- Does such-and-such a fictitious term, as used in the passage, necessarily imply the following meaning?

This is why "Critical Reading" is an appropriate term. You have the length of a Reading Comprehension passage, from which you'll need to draw Critical-Reasoning-like inferences. Yes, you have to draw inferences on regular RC, too, but IR raises the stakes. Occasionally, you will have to consider whether you have *sufficient data* to answer a question, much as on a Data Sufficiency question.

Sometimes, a small math task is explicitly blended into an essentially verbal challenge. Don't let that throw you—after all, the section is called "Integrated Reasoning"! Whatever the specific math/verbal breakdown of the content, you'll need to read through lots of information, organize it mentally, and make logical deductions.

Let's try an example of a Critical Reading task. Remember to follow good process:

1. Understand the prompt.
2. Understand the question.
3. Plan your approach.
4. Solve the problem.

Example Multi-Source Reasoning Prompt

As you read, ask yourself "What" and "So What."

Proposal | Purpose | Budget

The government of Storinia has proposed to conduct several particle physics experiments in Antarctica, as described below.

The *ultra-high-energy cosmic ray detector* (UHECR-D) will track a variety of subatomic particles traveling from outer space with exceptionally high kinetic energy by recording secondary showers of particles created by these UHECRs as they collide with the upper atmosphere.

The *polyethylene naphthalate neutrino observatory* (PEN-NO) will search for neutrinos, extremely light and fast subatomic particles that interact only weakly with normal matter. To prevent spurious results from cosmic rays, PEN-NO will be buried deep below the ice.

The *magnetic monopole detector* (MaMoD) will attempt to verify the existence of magnetic monopoles, hypothetical subatomic particles postulated by some physical theories to be left over from the creation of the universe.

Proposal | **Purpose** | Budget

The purpose of UHECR-D is to ascertain the identity, composition, and extraterrestrial origin of ultra-high-energy cosmic rays, which are much less prevalent and well-understood than lower-energy cosmic rays. PEN-NO will measure the mass and speed of neutrinos produced in particle accelerators and nuclear reactors, both to reduce uncertainty in the known mass of a neutrino and to contribute to the resolution of a recent challenge to Einstein's theory of relativity posed by the observation of neutrinos supposedly traveling slightly faster than light. PEN-NO will also measure the passage of solar and other neutrinos of astronomical origin. Finally, if MaMoD is successful in its search, it will provide experimental proof for Dirac's explanation of charge quantization and fix an asymmetry in Maxwell's equations of electromagnetism.

Proposal | Purpose | **Budget**

The government of Storinia projects that it will cost $42 million in total and take 2 years to construct UHECR-D, PEN-NO, and MaMoD. The government also projects that once construction is finished, the annual operating budget for each experiment will be $3.6 million for UHECR-D, $4.3 million for PEN-NO, and $2.7 million for MaMoD. All these figures are in real 2012 dollars (removing the effect of predicted inflation).

Example Questions

1. For each of the following statements, select Yes if the statement is supported by the evidence provided. Otherwise, select No.

Yes	No	
O	O	With a construction budget of $30 million, the Storinian government will be able to search for a proof of an explanation of charge quantization and to help resolve a controversy by measuring the speed of neutrinos produced in nuclear reactors.
O	O	In its Antarctic experiments, the Storinian government will attempt to ascertain the mass and speed of cosmic rays and to confirm the composition of magnetic monopoles.
O	O	If the PEN-NO experiment is kept in operation on the surface of the ice in Antarctica, its findings will be considered more valid than those produced by the experiment as currently envisioned.

2. According to the information provided, the proposed measurement of which of the following kinds of particles is intended to improve the quality of estimation of the mass of these particles?

  (A)   Ultra-high energy cosmic rays
  (B)   Particles created by UHECRs above the earth
  (C)   Neutrinos produced in nuclear reactors
  (D)   Neutrinos that originate in the sun
  (E)   Magnetic monopoles

3. For each of the following particle types, select Can Conclude if you can conclude from the information provided that the particles in question have a minimal effect on ordinary matter. Otherwise, select Cannot Conclude.

Can Conclude	Cannot Conclude	
O	O	Ultra-high-energy cosmic ray
O	O	Neutrinos produced in particle accelerators
O	O	Magnetic monopole

Solutions

Before getting to the solutions, consider the "What" and "So What" of the passage—the big picture and broad connections that you should look to grasp on your first reading.

First tab:

>**What:** Tells you that "Storinia" is planning 3 particle physics experiments in Antarctica.
>
>**So What:** Explains the 3 kinds of particles under investigation and in some cases how the experiments will work.

Second tab:

>**What:** Tells you the purpose of the 3 experiments.
>
>**So What:** Explains how each experiment could be important to physics—the broader "why" behind these experiments.

Third tab:

>**What:** Tells you the costs of the 3 experiments.
>
>**So What:** Provides a link between costs and purposes (in the second tab), so you can figure out how much it would cost to pursue various experimental goals.

1-a. No

Don't assume that the detectors cost an equal amount of money! Using letters for construction costs, you know that $U + P + M = \$42$ million, and also can assume that none of these amounts is $0 or less (positive costs are legitimate to assume). However, we can't conclude *anything* about $P + M$, other than $P + M$ is less than $42 million and greater than $0. Is $P + M$ less than or equal to $30 million? You don't know.

1-b. No

This statement is a classic case of word salad tossed for you fresh from the passage. You do not know whether the experiments will measure the "mass and speed of cosmic rays." What will the experiments do with cosmic rays? They will attempt to ascertain their identity, composition, and extraterrestrial origin—perhaps by measuring their mass and speed, in fact, but you are not told this.

Moreover, the experiments will attempt to verify the existence of magnetic monopoles, not confirm their composition, an intent that clearly implies that these particles have already been discovered. You know that they have *not* yet been discovered because they are called "hypothetical subatomic particles postulated by some physical theories."

1-c. No

The Proposal tab tells you that "to prevent spurious results from cosmic rays, PEN-NO will be buried deep below the ice." This text clearly implies that if PEN-NO is not buried in the ice (and is instead kept on the surface), there could be "spurious results from cosmic rays." "Spurious" means "extra, false, deceptive," so the overall results from PEN-NO would be considered less valid in this case, not more valid.

2. (C)

In the Purpose tab, you are told that "PEN-NO will measure the mass and speed of neutrinos produced in particle accelerators and nuclear reactors… to reduce uncertainty in the known mass of a neutrino…." To reduce uncertainty in this known mass is to improve the quality of estimation.

None of the other particle measurements specifically mention mass. All that is cited about "solar" neutrinos is that their "passage" will be measured; you do not know whether this measurement will ascertain the mass of these neutrinos.

3-a. Cannot Conclude

One thing that you know about ultra-high-energy cosmic rays is that they create "secondary showers of particles… as they collide with the upper atmosphere." So you cannot conclude that these UHECRs only have a minimal effect on ordinary matter. In fact, you would be able to conclude that these particles have an extreme effect on ordinary matter (notice that this conclusion is stronger than you need).

3-b. Can Conclude

In the Proposal tab, you are told that neutrinos are "extremely light and fast subatomic particles that interact only weakly with normal matter." In the second tab, a distinction is made between two sources of neutrinos, as to how these neutrinos will be measured and for what purpose. However, both kinds of neutrinos are neutrinos, so you can safely conclude that either kind has only a minimal effect on ordinary matter.

3-c. Cannot Conclude

You do not know what kind of effect these magnetic monopoles will have on ordinary matter. All you really know is that they are hypothetical and that if they are discovered, various theoretical implications will ensue.

Playing Little Logic Games

Occasionally, an Integrated Reasoning prompt poses a small logic puzzle involving a number of options and constraints. This sort of game doesn't really exist anywhere else on the GMAT, even in Critical Reasoning or on a quirky Word Problem.

If you are at all familiar with the LSAT (the law school admissions test), breathe easy—an IR logic puzzle is *much* simpler and shorter than an LSAT logic game. On IR, you might be asked to complete a short schedule, choosing from among several options by applying a few constraints and making some deductions.

Any individual constraint is straightforward. The most common kind is exclusion: if you have three pigeonholes and two are already filled with pigeons, you can only place one more pigeon (3 − 2 = 1) without doubling up. Two more pigeons simply won't fit. How might this idea play out in IR-land?

> A 7-day workweek at a tiny coffee shop needs one different worker on each day. No more than 5 workers can have the same gender. You already have 4 females and 1 male working. What are the possible genders of the remaining workers?

Think it through. You need 2 more people (7 − 5 = 2). If they're both male, you have 4 females and 3 males: fine. If one's male and one's female, then you have 5 females and 2 males: also fine. But you can't have 2 additional females, or you'll be over the limit. So you have to have at least one more male worker.

Believe it or not, that simple pigeonhole principle will take you a long way. The hard part isn't dealing with any single constraint; it's dealing with *several* constraints. Don't panic! Just knock them down one by one. Of course, first make sure that you understand the prompt and the question. Then follow the logic. Complicated constraints will boil down to simpler search parameters that you can apply to the answer choices.

As you consider the answer choices, work from wrong to right. Look for easy knockouts first. Can you get rid of any options quickly? You probably can.

These problems can all be solved in a reasonable amount of time (a couple of minutes, roughly) and with a reasonable amount of effort. They look scary on their face, but remember that there will be "smoke and mirrors"—distracting content that will fall away as you proceed, ultimately contributing nothing to the answer. These problems have a loud bark, but not too bad of a bite, as long as you don't let the noise startle you.

Let's try an example.

Example "Little Logic Game" Problem and Question

4. A chemical plant operating continuously has two 12-hour shifts, a day shift and a night shift, during each of which as many as five chemicals can be produced. Equipment limitations and safety regulations impose constraints on the types of chemicals that can be produced during the same shift. No more than two oxidizers can be produced per shift; the same limit holds true for monomers. On either shift, the sum of fire protection standards for all chemicals should be no greater than 13 for health risk, 12 for flammability, and 9 for reactivity. On each of these three dimensions, the standard for any chemical is an integer that ranges from 0 (lowest) to 4 (highest).

Four chemicals have already been chosen for each shift, as shown below:

⑬ HR   ⑫ F   ⑨ R

Day shift

Acrylonitrile	(health = 4, flammability = 3, reactivity = 2, oxidizer = no, monomer = yes)
Chloroprene	(health = 2, flammability = 3, reactivity = 0, oxidizer = no, monomer = yes)
Hydrogen peroxide	(health = 3, flammability = 0, reactivity = 2, oxidizer = yes, monomer = no)
Titanium dioxide	(health = 1, flammability = 0, reactivity = 0, oxidizer = no, monomer = no)

10   6   4

Night shift

Ammonium nitrate	(health = 2, flammability = 0, reactivity = 3, oxidizer = yes, monomer = no)
Phosphine	(health = 4, flammability = 4, reactivity = 2, oxidizer = no, monomer = no)
Potassium perchlorate	(health = 1, flammability = 0, reactivity = 1, oxidizer = yes, monomer = no)
Propylene	(health = 1, flammability = 4, reactivity = 1, oxidizer = no, monomer = yes)

8   8   7

Select a chemical that could be added to either shift. Then select a chemical that could be added to neither shift. Make only two selections, one in each column.

Either shift	Neither shift	Chemical
O	O	Chlorine (health = 3, flammability = 0, reactivity = 0, oxidizer = yes, monomer = no) ✗
O	O	Ethylene (health = 3, flammability = 4, reactivity = 2, oxidizer = no, monomer = yes)
O	●	Nickel carbonyl (health = 4, flammability = 3, reactivity = 3, oxidizer = no, monomer = no) ✗
●	O	Phenol (health = 3, flammability = 2, reactivity = 0, oxidizer = no, monomer = no)
O	O	Sulfuric acid (health = 3, flammability = 0, reactivity = 2, oxidizer = yes, monomer = no) ✗
O	O	Vinyl chloride (health = 2, flammability = 4, reactivity = 2, oxidizer = no, monomer = yes) ✗

Solution

3

4. As always, the first two steps are to understand the prompt and to understand the question. Take your time!

You are given information about the two work shifts of a chemical plant, day and night. At most five chemicals can be produced during either shift. Four of the five slots on each shift are already filled, so you're looking to fill the fifth slot.

Not just any chemical can fill the fifth slot, though. You are given several constraints:

- No more than 2 "oxidizers" (whatever they are) per shift.
- No more than 2 "monomers" (ditto) per shift.
- Health numbers add up to 13 or less.
- Flammability numbers add up to 12 or less.
- Reactivity numbers add up to 9 or less.
- For any chemical, any one of these numbers could be 0, 1, 2, 3, or 4.

Notice that you have to do a little light translating as you go, in order to make the concepts more tangible.

What are you asked for? In this two-part question, you are asked to identify a single chemical that would fit *either* shift (there's only one) and another chemical that would fit *neither* shift (again, there's only one). The characteristics of each chemical in the list of six to choose from will make all the difference, obviously.

Now what? Plan your approach. Since this problem is about following a chain of logic, go ahead and figure out what *must* and *must not* be true about the fifth chemical, by applying the given constraints to the four chemicals you already have. Do this for each shift. Then, armed with new and *simpler* constraints about the fifth possibility for each shift, go through the list of six chemicals and figure out whether the chemical in question could be on the shift. One chemical could go on either; another chemical could go on neither; the other four chemicals will go on one but not the other. Hopefully, you'll be able to go quickly at that stage.

Finally, execute your plan to solve the problem.

Day: You already have two monomers, the most you're allowed to have, so the last chemical can't be a monomer. That's one constraint. You can have an oxidizer (or not). The health numbers add up to 10, and you can have 13 at most, so the biggest possible health number for the last chemical is 3. That is, the last chemical can't have a health of 4. Flammability adds up to 6, and the cap is 12, so you can have any flammability (the maximum flammability is 4). Likewise, you can have any reactivity (the numbers only add to 4, and the cap is 9). Thus:

Day constraints: Can't have health = 4. Can't be a monomer. Anything else goes.

See how these new constraints look much easier to apply to the list of chemicals?

Night: You already have two oxidizers, the most you're allowed to have, so the last chemical can't be an oxidizer (but it could be a monomer, or not). The numbers add up differently. Here, you can have any health number (cap of 13 − sum of 8 = room for up to 5) or any flammability number (cap of 12 − sum of 8 = room for up to 4). However, the reactivity number cannot be 3 or 4, since the cap is 9 and the other numbers add to 7, leaving room only for a 0, 1, or 2 for the last chemical. Thus:

> Night constraints: Can't have reactivity = 3 or 4. Can't be an oxidizer. Anything else goes.

Now apply these constraints to the list of six chemicals. See whether you can accelerate your thinking at this point, rather than go through all 12 options (each chemical for each shift) laboriously. Can you knock out any possible answers easily?

For instance, consider the "either" answer. What must be true about that chemical? Well, a chemical that could go on *either* shift must be neither an oxidizer nor a monomer, since each of those types is knocked out on one or the other of the shifts. So you can knock out four chemicals quickly, leaving nickel carbonyl and phenol (which are both "no-no's" on the oxidizer and monomer scales).

Which of these two chemicals is more likely to work on either shift? Phenol has lower numbers, so it's more likely to fit. In fact, its health number is low enough (3) to fit the day shift, and its reactivity number is low enough (2) to fit the night shift. Phenol is the "either" answer.

Having just looked at nickel carbonyl, you might reconsider it. Its numbers are pretty high all around: 4, 3, and 3. The day shift rules out a health number of 4, while the night shift rules out a reactivity number of 3. So this chemical turns out to be the "neither" answer. Thus:

> **Either shift: phenol   Neither shift: nickel carbonyl**

At this point on an actual exam, make your selections and move on. Do not waste time proving the possible shift locations of every other chemical. During review, of course, it's worth it to practice following the logic quickly. So that you can check your work, here are the other results:

> Chlorine: day only (no more oxidizers at night)
> Ethylene: night only (no more monomers during the day)
> Sulfuric acid: day only (no more oxidizers at night)
> Vinyl chloride: night only (no more monomers during the day)

Interpreting Real-World Communications

Integrated Reasoning	GMAT Verbal
Includes **real-world** communications	Usually just plain exposition from an un-named author to reader
• **Dialogues** or exchanges that reflect social relationships • **Two or three stages** in the dialogue, like an elaborate comic strip	• Descriptions and explanations • Arguments for a position
Mgr: "Is the project done?" *Staff:* "It will be, next week." *Mgr:* "Do you like your job?"	"Within its mountain habi-tat, the two-tailed eagle can be considered both an apex predator and a scavenger...."

From time to time, Critical Reasoning on GMAT Verbal includes a dialogue or names the speaker *Advocate, Mayor,* etc. However, this "social" aspect of GMAT Verbal is very minor.

In contrast, Integrated Reasoning tests how well you **interpret common interactions** in the business world, as they are expressed through **dialogues**.

To perform well on dialogue-interpretation questions, you will have to pick up on subtle nuances in the way that something is said. Examine these three sentences and determine the degree of willingness expressed:

> President: "We should not violate the treaty."
> President: "We should try not to violate the treaty."
> President: "We should not try to violate the treaty."

In the first version, the president is *unwilling* to violate the treaty, saying that doing so would be *wrong*. In the second version, the little words "*try not to*" soften the stance in a critical way. Now the president is *willing* to violate the treaty if necessary, although doing so may still be regrettable. The third version is slightly different from either of the other two: what's bad is *trying* to violate the treaty (and not trying may be enough to prevent violation), but it may be okay to violate the treaty by accident.

Likewise, **expectations** can be conveyed by a single word—or even by the fact that something was said at all. When expectations clash with reality, pay attention! For example:

> Version A   *Friend:* "You're here."
>   = You are now here. You *weren't* here before.
>   (Otherwise, why would I bring it up?)

Version B	Friend: "You're already here."
	= You are now here. You *weren't* here before. I expected you
	not to be here now. I expected you to be here *later*.
Version C	Friend: "You're still here."
	= You are now here. You *were* here before. I expected you *not*
	to be here by now.

These nuances may make all the difference in the communication, whether international relations, interpersonal relationships, or Integrated Reasoning is at stake.

Social Relationships in Integrated Reasoning

A wife says to her husband, "Are you going to take out the garbage?" Describe the meaning of each of the following possible responses, in as many ways as you can:

(a) *Husband:* "Are you going to give me a kiss?"

(b) *Husband:* "Are you going to wash the dishes?"

(c) *Husband:* "Are you going to stop asking me?"

Let's come back to this exercise. In the meantime, think about how hard or easy it was to do. Dialogue interpretation will be natural for some and not for others. Those who automatically read between the lines will find this material more straightforward than those who are very literal in their interpretations. The second group will need to master and apply a framework, such as the one that follows.

How to Interpret a Dialogue

As you read an email exchange on IR, ask yourself two questions:

1. **Who are these people?**
2. If each email is a move in a social game, **what is the purpose of each move?**

If you already pick up this kind of stuff unconsciously and effectively… great! Don't mess with success. But if you sometimes miss nuances in interactions, ask these questions *consciously*.

When you ask *Who are these people?*, you're really asking about their relationship. What does each side usually want? What is their relative power? What do you expect to happen in an interaction?

Work environments are somewhat culturally determined, so IR will focus on business relationships that are likely to be common across cultures and that represent environments found within typical b-schools and employers. Here are a few such relationships and associated power dynamics:

1.   Relationships within a company or other organization:

a. Boss – Employee

The boss can direct the activity of the employee for the good of the company, within the course of normal employment. Power can manifest itself in different ways: some boss-employee relationships are "command and control," while others are more collaborative and permissive. Employees have rights and can even quit, but the boss is the one who hires and fires.

b. Colleague – Colleague

Neither party has direct power over the other. Rather, they are expected to work together for the common good of their employer. If the two sides disagree, they will be expected to resolve the conflict as long as they remain employed.

2)   Inside-outside relationships between someone inside the company and someone on the outside:

a. Customer – Salesperson

The salesperson wants the customer to buy. The customer has the power to walk away and so in theory has more power.

Variations include **client – advisor** (fancier, longer-term, less transactional), **customer – support staff** (customer has already purchased but still has need), and **buyer – vendor** (now the company is the customer in a business-to-business relationship).

b. Job applicant – Recruiter

The applicant wants the job. The recruiter may seem to be in the driver's seat, but the company also needs great staff, and the applicant may be weighing other offers. In this case, the applicant may have the upper hand. Both sides can walk away from the negotiation.

c. Executive – Other stakeholder

Businesses operate within society. For instance, a CEO may have to interact with a regulator or with a citizen in a town where the company has a plant.

It's important to consider *normal expectations* for the relationship. Normal expectations are what permit meaningful omissions in the dialogue. Not everything has to be said explicitly in a relationship. Whatever is *not* said must accord with normal expectations.

The second big question to ask is about the specific content of the dialogue. Analyze each communication in a dialogue as a *move in a game*. What is the purpose of the move?

Simply put, **words are actions**. When you examine someone's words in an IR dialogue, think: **What is he or she doing *by* saying these words?**

Imagine that you're reading an email from Joe to Sandy. Every sentence in the email operates on at least one of three levels:

1. Facts   2. Wants   3. Emotions

The email as a whole operates on all three levels at once. Let's look at each in turn:

1. **Facts**
    - What is the factual content of the text? What ideas, perspectives, and opinions are in there? Analyze the text as a ***statement or question about the world***.
    - On this level, Joe can be doing the following things:
        - **Describe, assert, predict, explain, guess, wonder, express an expectation or belief,** etc.
        Joe says something about the world, now or in the future, with some degree of certainty or uncertainty. This may or may not reflect what Joe really thinks.
        - **Ask about, inquire**, etc.
        Joe inquires about Sandy's ideas and opinions, in order to get them out in the open.
        - **Agree about, disagree about, affirm, refute, contradict, ignore, emphasize,** etc.
        In response to Sandy's perspectives, Joe reveals his own take on the facts (or the take he wants to reveal) and his degree of agreement or disagreement with Sandy. He may ignore or emphasize some portions of Sandy's previous communications.

2. **Wants**
    - What does the text indicate about what Joe wants and how he's trying to get it? How is he responding to what Sandy wants? Analyze the text as an exertion of power.
    - On this level, Joe can be doing the following things:
        - **Commit, promise, offer, agree to, acquiesce, refuse, permit,** etc.
        Joe states his own intentions and desires about an action clearly within his own control. This may or may not be in response to a request or demand from Sandy. Explicitly or not, Joe is expressing his willingness or unwillingness.
        - **Ask for, request, demand, plead, invite, command, forbid, warn,** etc.
        Joe wants Sandy to do something and is trying to get her to do it, with varying degrees of politeness, candor, and force.

3. **Emotions**
    - What emotions is Joe conveying, and how are they in reaction to what has come before? Is Joe trying to change Sandy's emotional state, and if so, how? Analyze the text as an ***expression of feelings***.
    - On this level, Joe can be doing the following things:

- **Thank, congratulate, praise, blame, criticize, wish well or ill, commiserate, soothe, encourage, discourage,** etc.

    Joe explicitly directs his emotion towards Sandy.

- **Express his own happiness, sorrow, anger, joy, resignation, excitement,** etc.

    Joe indicates or implies how he feels about something. His emotion may still be directed toward Sandy, but in a more implicit or even unconscious way. In fact, his emotion may not be directed toward her at all.

Even a short communication can hit on all three levels. Typically, the level of facts is most explicit in the text; the deeper levels of wants and emotions are often implied in the **subtext**. However, the wants and emotions form just as much a part of the meaning as the facts do.

 Joe to Sandy: "Great job on yesterday's presentation! Sam told me he was impressed. I'll follow up with Rachel later today."

Facts	Joe **describes** the presentation as great. He also **reports** that Sam was impressed. Joe finally **predicts** that he will follow up with Rachel later today.
Wants	Joe **promises** to follow up with Rachel later today. Joe also **wants** Sandy to feel good about the work.
Emotions	Joe **congratulates** Sandy on a job well done and **expresses** his happiness.

If you tend to think very literally, you might register the fact level and miss the levels of wants and emotions:

Alice: "Are you going to eat the rest of that sandwich?"

Bob: "No, I'm not."

Silence.

What Bob missed is that Alice was not just asking *whether* Bob was going to eat the sandwich. She was asking *for* it (although only if Bob wasn't going to eat it).

Another kind of miscommunication arises when emotions run high. If you and I are in a fight, I'll insist that my questions and statements should only be taken at "face" value (the level of facts), even though I meant them to have loaded subtext. Meanwhile, I'm reading into everything *you* say at the level of wants and emotions (and granting those aspects the most weight). You're doing all the same things back to me, insisting that *your* utterances are only factual but that *my* utterances are primarily about wants and emotions.

Finally, it can be helpful to consider what is NOT said, relative to our expectations for the typical relationship:

 Employee: "Can I work from home on Friday?"

 Boss: "Email me every hour with an update."

The subtext is that the boss is saying *Yes* (although in a grudging way). The "Yes" is not explicit, but you can infer it. For one thing, the command assumes that the employee will be home to carry it out. Also, the expectations for a boss-employee relationship are that the boss will make a decision and answer. A "No" or "Maybe" would need to be more explicit. The boss grants permission implicitly.

Let's return to the exchange between wife and husband, from the beginning of this section:

 Wife: "Are you going to take out the garbage?"

Husband: "Are you going to give me a kiss?"

The wife is not just asking a Yes/No question to wonder about the future; she is really asking her husband to do the task. It's not out of the blue, either—she is probably reminding him (the "are you going to" construction implies that it was expected for him to take out the garbage).

In response, the husband poses another Yes/No question about the future on the level of Facts: whether she will give him a kiss. On the level of Wants, he invites her to kiss him. His request is easy to fulfill and is focused on a sign of affection, so he's really saying *Yes* in a nice way, if slightly edgy. He is willing to take the garbage out. The subtext might be expressed this way:

Husband: *Yes, of course! Just give me a little kiss, and I'll take the garbage out.*

Consider the second example:

Wife: "Are you going to take out the garbage?"

Husband: "Are you going to wash the dishes?"

Now the husband's request is not as easy to fulfill and is focused on another domestic chore. He may be offering a trade or criticizing her back. The emotional tone is harsher than before. He is only willing to take the garbage out under certain circumstances.

Husband: *Maybe I haven't taken out the garbage as expected, but you haven't washed the dishes as expected, so there. I'll take out the garbage as soon as you wash the dishes.*

Now consider the third example:

 Wife: "Are you going to take out the garbage?"

 Husband: "Are you going to stop asking me?"

This response expresses real anger. It's unclear whether the husband is actually *willing* to take the garbage out, but he is certainly pushing back on his wife. The emotional tone is clearly negative:

 Husband: *Stop asking me about the garbage. You have asked me too many times already. This issue really upsets me.*

It's unlikely that you'll read such an emotionally charged dialogue on the IR section—for one thing, it's too memorable! But you should practice picking up on the subtext of dialogues, in particular around expectations, wants, and emotions.

Example Communications Problems

Read each of the following short dialogues. What is each person saying (or might be saying) at the level of facts, wants, and emotions? How does the context of the relationship affect your interpretation of the dialogue?

5. Worker: "How can I possibly get these TPS reports done by 2pm?"
Co-worker: "Would it make sense to bring someone else in on the process at this late stage?"

	Worker	Co-worker
Facts		
Wants		
Emotions		

6. Potential vendor: "What else can we do to win your business?"
Buyer: "What are you implying?"

	Vendor	Buyer
Facts		
Wants		
Emotions		

7. Mining company executive: "Isn't it possible that the groundwater pollution stems from natural causes?"
Local mayor: "Can you show me the results of the groundwater testing that was legally supposed to be performed this year?"

	Executive	Mayor
Facts		
Wants		
Emotions		

Solutions

5. Worker: "How can I possibly get these TPS reports done by 2pm?"
Co-worker: "Would it make sense to bring someone else in on the process at this late stage?"

Worker:

Facts	The worker asks how he/she can get these reports done by 2pm.
Wants	The worker wants the co-worker to empathize, if nothing else, and possibly to offer or find assistance.
Emotions	The worker expresses frustration with the situation (emphasized by the word "possibly"). The question is really rhetorical; this person is probably complaining, not asking for an answer.

Co-worker:

Facts	The co-worker asks whether it would make sense to bring in a helper ("someone else in on the process") at this point. The co-worker deliberately doesn't answer the other person's question as it was stated.
Wants	The co-worker could be *just asking* (to get the first speaker to think of solutions), or *offering* to help out (directly or indirectly), or even *questioning* the value of additional help (and thereby deflecting any subtle request for help). The word "late" is loaded and can cut either way; it could emphasize that help is now futile or that it's now more necessary than ever.
Emotions	The co-worker could be expressing sympathy or criticism (or both). The co-worker does not directly answer the question (meaning that he/she gets that the first speaker is asking a rhetorical question). Again, "late" is a loaded word that most likely carries judgment of some kind.

The two speakers are colleagues; the second speaker does not have formal authority over the first. Thus, the first speaker could just be venting to the co-worker, whose response is not a command but rather a suggestion.

Notice how different the second question would be if the co-worker leads with "*Wouldn't* it make sense…." In that case, the clear implication is that it *would* make sense to bring someone else in (the co-worker or someone else). This response would be more directive.

6. Potential vendor: "What else can we do to win your business?"
Buyer: "What are you implying?"

Vendor:

Facts	The vendor is asking what else can be done to win the buyer's business.
Wants	The vendor wants the buyer to continue to consider the possibility of a deal. The vendor is offering to do something more to get the deal done. "Else" implies that something valuable has already been offered.
Emotions	From the words themselves, the vendor's emotions are hard to read. Most likely, the sentence would be read straight, at face value. However, there could be a sense of conspiracy under the surface, a willingness to do something underhanded for the buyer. It depends on what has already been offered, for one thing.

3

Buyer:

Facts	The buyer ignores the vendor's question and asks what the vendor is implying. In this way, the *buyer* is implying something: namely, that the vendor's question has an unstated implication, and that this implication is nefarious (otherwise it would be stated outright, not implied).
Wants	The buyer wants to cut off any possibility that the conversation could be interpreted in an illicit light. The buyer wants the vendor to back off, and in fact is probably closing the door to any future business relationship.
Emotions	The buyer reacts very negatively—practically accusing the vendor of attempted bribery.

The two speakers are supposedly in an arm's-length business relationship, in which the vendor is trying to sell to the buyer, who is negotiating on behalf of his or her company. The responsibility that the buyer has to his or her employer (together with the potential for abuse) is what sparks the buyer's reaction. If this dialogue occurred between a salesperson and a customer negotiating only on his or her own behalf, the "nefarious" implication would be less obvious.

7. Mining company executive: "Isn't it possible that the groundwater pollution stems from natural causes?"
Local mayor: "Can you show me the results of the groundwater testing that was legally supposed to be performed this year?"

Executive:

Facts	The executive asks whether it's impossible for the groundwater pollution to stem from natural causes. The phrasing "the groundwater pollution" implies that this issue has already been mentioned ("the" means "you know what I'm talking about") and that whatever has happened *is* actually groundwater pollution: the executive is not disputing the presence of pollution, simply its cause.

Wants	The executive wants the mayor to consider an alternative cause and thereby to weaken the implication that the company is at fault for the pollution. With the phrasing "*isn't* it possible…" (versus "*is* it possible"), the executive implies that this alternative cause is, in fact, very possible.
Emotions	On its surface, the executive's phrasing reflects reasonability. He or she doesn't *state* that the pollution could have resulted from natural causes; rather, he or she *asks* whether it's not possible that such is the case. Of course, in a spoken dialogue, a host of verbal and non-verbal cues (e.g., tone, volume, facial expressions) would either support or undermine this impression of reasonability in the words themselves.

Mayor:

Facts	As in the previous dialogues, the mayor sidesteps the posed question and asks whether the executive can produce the results of groundwater testing that was to be performed this year.
Wants	The mayor wants the executive to produce these results. By using the word "legally," the mayor reinforces his or her stance that the testing was to have been done this year (implying that the results should be released). At another level, the mayor wants to take this conversation to a different place; he or she doesn't want to debate whether a particular cause may or may not be possible. The mayor sends this message clearly by ignoring the posed question.
Emotions	The mayor demonstrates some frustration or at least willingness to spar with the executive by ignoring the executive's question and posing another (which is really a demand for an item).

A company executive and a local mayor (of a town where the company operates) have explicit authority over different spheres of society. These two people probably have a complicated relationship. The company provides jobs, but the company's operations may have adverse effects on the local population. The mayor is clearly taking a combative stance with the executive, perhaps defending (or appearing to defend) the town against such adverse effects.

Chapter 4 *of* Integrated Reasoning

IR Preparation and Review

In This Chapter...

Chapter 4:
IR Preparation and Review

Now that you've read the previous chapters and done example problems along the way, it's time to log on and do more practice online.

Integrated Reasoning is not computer-adaptive, but the new prompt and question formats, such as sortable tables, are very "computer-enabled." To get a real feel for these problems, you have to face them in their native environment — on a computer. After all, you can't learn a program such as Excel by reading a book — you have to play with the program live.

There are plenty of online problems for you to practice with. If you're a student in one of our classes or working with one of our tutors, log in to your Student Center. If you've bought this book separately, go to page 7 and follow the instructions for registering your purchase and accessing online resources.

How to Prepare for the IR Section

First, do the Integrated Reasoning question banks that we provide in the Student Center. Each of these banks is specific to one of the four prompt types. Within these banks, you'll encounter a variety of question types, from traditional multiple-choice to the newer formats. Be sure to use the onscreen calculator provided. After each bank, closely review the explanations for all problems, not just the ones that you got wrong or took a lot of time to complete.

Of course, do practice problems that GMAC has released publicly. Some are available for free on mba.com as examples to illustrate the new section. Actually solve these problems — don't just read through them and skip to the answer. You should also work through the 50 practice problems that the GMAT folks include with *The Official Guide for GMAT Review, 13th Edition* (in an online supplement).

Next, do full GMAT practice exams with the IR section. The very first time you do a practice exam, you might skip IR, along with the essay. This way, you won't be distracted by these less important sections as you focus on the crucial GMAT Quant and GMAT Verbal portions of the exam. However, on your subsequent exams, you should definitely include the IR section, even if you continue to skip the essay. Take these tests under normal exam-like conditions: time limits, etc. The more that your practice tests feel like the GMAT, the better prepared you'll be. (For that matter, be sure to do at least one practice exam with the essay included.) You can do our practice exams (included with this book) as well as GMAT Prep, the practice exams supplied by GMAC.

Finally, stay focused on the GMAT Quant and GMAT Verbal sections. The core skills are largely the same: doing percent computations, reading a passage closely, and so on. The context and feel are different, but if you master percents, for instance, you can apply your mastery both on GMAT Quant and on IR. Don't over-stress about the IR section as a separate entity.

On the next few pages are summaries of the IR material covered in this book.

IR Summaries

What Is Integrated Reasoning?

Logistics:

- 30-minute section between the essay and GMAT Quant
- Separately scored—much less important than the main 200–800 score
- 12 prompts with 1 or more questions per prompt
- New formats of prompts and questions
  - Some prompts are interactive
  - New questions require 2–3 responses per question
- Non-adaptive, but you can't go backwards
- Calculator provided (for this section only)

Purpose:

- Exposure to b-school case analysis, in miniature
  - Integrates math and verbal thinking
  - Hits you with a flood of real-world data
- Content is largely the same as on GMAT Quant and Verbal
  - Challenge: time pressure, new formats

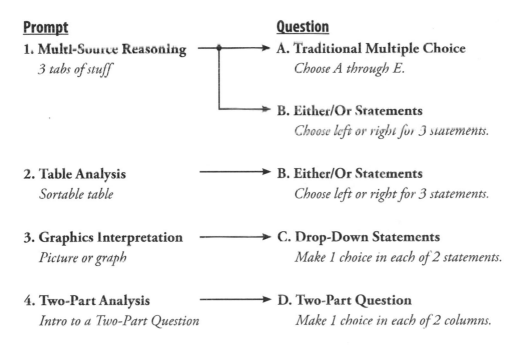

Prompt

1. Multi-Source Reasoning
3 tabs of stuff

2. Table Analysis
Sortable table

3. Graphics Interpretation
Picture or graph

4. Two-Part Analysis
Intro to a Two-Part Question

Question

A. Traditional Multiple Choice
Choose A through E.

B. Either/Or Statements
Choose left or right for 3 statements.

B. Either/Or Statements
Choose left or right for 3 statements.

C. Drop-Down Statements
Make 1 choice in each of 2 statements.

D. Two-Part Question
Make 1 choice in each of 2 columns.

How Do I Deal with IR during the GMAT?

Don't let IR mess up the rest of your test:
- Build stamina and speed in advance; drink a Gatorade during the break.

Make small but critical adjustments after IR, as you transition into GMAT Quant and Verbal:
- It's okay to give up using the calculator, because Quant numbers are rigged.
- A lot less extra information will be provided in Quant questions.
- Stop reading as much between the lines on Verbal prompts.

What Process Should I Follow on an IR Problem?

1. Understand the prompt:
- Ask yourself *What* and *So What* to build a fast, high-level mental map.

2. Understand the question:
- Take your time and focus on the precise language. Don't go overboard.

3. Plan your approach:
- The best way forward = the easiest and most obvious to you.
- Draw on your knowledge of similar problems.

4. Solve the problem:
- Write things down. Articulate to yourself what you're doing.
- Use the calculator provided to handle messy numbers.
- Challenge your logic by playing devil's advocate.

IR Quant

Tables and Graphs

Don't be put off by the variety of formats and the amount of data. You will be able to figure out anything they throw at you. Review the graph zoo in Chapter 2 for reassurance.

Read the title and the labels. Focus on one part at a time. Literally point at the screen. In a scatterplot, each point is a pair of numbers (x and y) corresponding to one case.

Percents, Decimals, Ratios

Common Percent Translations

$$x\% \text{ of } y = \left(\frac{x}{100}\right)y \qquad x\% \text{ more than } y = \left(1 + \frac{x}{100}\right)y \qquad \text{What percent is } k \text{ of } m? \ \left(\frac{k}{m}\right) \times 100\%$$

$$20\% \text{ more than } z = \text{Increase } z \text{ by } 20\% = \left(1 + \frac{20}{100}\right)z = 1.2z$$

$$30\% \text{ less than } w = \text{Decrease } w \text{ by } 30\% = \left(1 - \frac{30}{100}\right)w = 0.7w$$

$$\text{What percent is } k \text{ more than } m? \ \left(\frac{k - m}{m}\right) \times 100\% = \left(\frac{k}{m} - 1\right) \times 100\%$$

$$\text{Percent change from Old to New} = \left(\frac{\text{New} - \text{Old}}{\text{Old}}\right) \times 100\% = \left(\frac{\text{New}}{\text{Old}} - 1\right) \times 100\%$$

Decrease x by 20%, then increase the result by 25%. You are back to x! $(0.80)(1.25)x = \left(\dfrac{4}{5}\right)\left(\dfrac{5}{4}\right)x = x$

Common FDP Traps

Percents vs. Quantities (e.g., dollars)—don't mix these up as you read a chart!
　　Portfolio A has a greater % of its money in stocks than Portfolio B does.
　　But Portfolio A may or may not have more actual *dollars* in stocks than Portfolio B does.

Percent of What—pay attention to what you're taking a percent of:
　　"Oil imports from Brazil, as a percent of all imports" is not the same as "oil imports
　　from Brazil, as a percent of all OIL imports."

$$\frac{\text{Oil imports from Brazil}}{\text{All imports}} = \frac{\text{Oil imports from Brazil}}{\text{All OIL imports}} \times \frac{\text{All OIL imports}}{\text{All imports}}$$

Ratio of What to What—pay attention to how variables or units cancel in ratios:

Miles per gallon equals miles per hour, times hours per gallon. $\dfrac{\text{Miles}}{\text{Gallon}} = \dfrac{\text{Miles}}{\text{Hour}} \times \dfrac{\text{Hours}}{\text{Gallon}}$

Statistics

Measures of the Center of Data

$$\text{Average} = \text{Mean} = \text{Arithmetic Mean} = \frac{\text{Sum of numbers}}{\text{Number of numbers}}$$

Median = middle number, 50th percentile (half of the cases are above, half are below):

       25th percentile = 25% of the numbers are below this number

       75th percentile = 75% of the numbers are below this number

Mode = most common number (highest frequency)

Measures of the Spread of Data

Range = largest number − smallest number (very affected by outliers)

Standard Deviation acts a lot like the average of the absolute distance between the mean and each number.

Most of the data lies within 2 standard deviations of the mean, for bell curves such as the normal distribution.

Variance = the square of the standard deviation

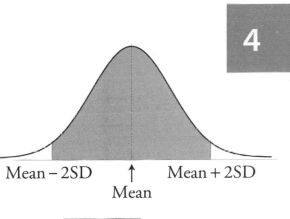

Mean − 2SD   ↑   Mean + 2SD

              Mean

Correlation between Two Columns of Data, X and Y

Positive correlation or relationship:

       Both variables tend to rise or fall together.

       Best-fit regression line through scatterplot has positive slope.

Negative correlation:

       When one variable increases, the other tends to decrease.

       Best-fit line through scatterplot has negative slope.

No correlation:

       Scatterplot doesn't reveal any linear pattern.

IR Verbal

"Critical Reading"—required by Integrated Reasoning prompts with a lot of text:

- Critical Reading = Reading Comprehension + a little Critical Reasoning (+ even a little Data Sufficiency)
- Draw logical inferences carefully. Be ready to conclude that you *don't* have enough information.

Little Logic Games—occasionally you must play a little game involving options and constraints:

- Follow the logic for each constraint. Turn the given constraints into simple search criteria. Look for quick knockouts among the answer choices. These games look worse than they are.

Real-World Communications—occasionally you must interpret a dialogue (e.g., an email exchange):

- Pay attention to nuances that indicate willingness and expectations.
- Ask yourself "Who are these people?" and "What is the purpose of each communication?"
- Analyze each communication on 3 levels: facts, wants, and emotions.

Chapter 5 of Integrated Reasoning

The Argument Essay

In This Chapter...

Chapter 5:
The Argument Essay

The GMAT begins with its most open-ended task: the Analytical Writing Assessment (AWA), also known as the Argument Essay, or just the essay. Some folks will find this task straightforward. Others will find it challenging. Either way, you need to familiarize yourself with this piece of the GMAT.

What Is the Argument Essay?

This section of the GMAT consists of one 30-minute essay that you type into the computer. In this essay, you'll examine a flawed argument.

The essay is separately scored—it does not factor into your general GMAT score (200–800). The scale runs from 0 (lowest) to 6 (highest) in half-point increments. You'll be assessed on two sets of skills:

1. *Logical analysis:* how well do you dissect and evaluate the argument?
2. *Persuasive writing:* how clearly and convincingly do you express your thoughts?

Chapter 11 of *The Official Guide for GMAT Review, 13th Edition* describes the essay task and provides a few useful example essays, as well as other material worth scanning. In an appendix, the OG also outlines the AWA scoring scale and corresponding percentiles of a large set of recent test-takers.

AWA Score	Label	Percentile
6.0	Outstanding	91
5.5		77
5.0	Strong	57
4.5		38
4.0	Adequate	20
3.5		10
3.0	Limited	6
2.5		4
2.0	Seriously Flawed	3
1.5		3
1.0	Fundamentally Deficient	3
0.5		3
0.0	No Score	0

A 6.0 essay "presents a cogent, well-articulated critique of the argument and demonstrates mastery of the elements of effective writing," though there may still be minor flaws. At the other end of the spectrum, *No score* means you've left the essay blank, written something off topic or in a language other than English (including gibberish), or just recopied the topic. To get a 0.0, you have to thumb your nose deliberately at the GMAT.

Performance of Test-Takers

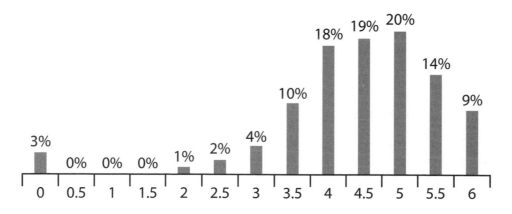

Notice that 80% of test-takers score "Adequate" (4.0) or better, while nearly half (43%) score "Strong" (5.0) or better. Both a computer and a human (or two) grade your essay, so you'll receive your AWA score later, when you receive your official scores from GMAC.

What is the purpose of this essay in the admissions process?

It is *not* to distinguish exceptional performance from strong or even adequate performance. An "Outstanding" essay will not improve your admissions chances more than a "Strong" essay will.

In a March 2011 research report, the GMAT folks admit that for the general population of applicants, AWA scores add very little to the power of the GMAT and undergraduate grades to predict academic performance in business school.

So why is this essay on the GMAT? **To catch the bottom 20% of scores.**

The schools want to ensure that you can write English well enough to handle graduate-level academic coursework conducted in English, particularly if you are a non-native speaker. And this essay is the only thing that schools know that you wrote completely on your own. The AWA score provides admissions officers with a "Fine" or "Not Fine" on your ability to write in English.

Here are school reactions to AWA scores:

Score	Label	Percent of Test-Takers	School Reaction
6.0	Outstanding	9%	"Good enough!"
5.5		14%	
5.0	Strong	20%	"Good enough!"
4.5		19%	
4.0	Adequate	18%	"Probably fine!"
3.5		10%	"Umm, less fine…."
3.0	Limited	4%	
2.5		2%	
2.0	Seriously Flawed	1%	"Who wrote the applicaiton essays?"
1.5		0%	
1.0	Fundamentally Deficient	0%	
0.5		0%	
0.0	No Score	3%	

In short, getting a low score (bottom 20%) on the essay can hurt your chances of admission.

At the top end of the scale, a 5.5 may dissatisfy you. Do not let it do so!

Your goal on the essay should be to clear the bar cleanly with a 4.5 or higher.

What about a 4.0? This score is probably fine for admission to any school. After all, a 4.0 is labeled "Adequate." You've just cleared the bar, but the schools don't really care about how much you clear the bar by. If you get a 4.0, should you retake the GMAT just to improve to a 4.5? Almost certainly not.

That said, if you're going to retake the GMAT anyway, you should put in a little more time on AWA preparation, so that you clear the hurdle with a little more room. And if you're at all worried about how the schools are going to perceive your facility with academic English, then a 4.5 or better can help set your (and their) mind at ease.

By the way, schools will be able to read your actual essay. Don't let this fact quicken your pulse—schools will likely not bother to read the essay unless the score is low. Admissions officers are incredibly overworked. They know that moderate to high AWA scores yield slight information. And the essay itself is not going to give brilliant new insights into your thinking or character.

Last but not least, any admissions officer who *does* happen to read your essay will recognize that you only have 30 minutes to plan the task and write on an artificial topic not of your choosing. In its directions on how to use AWA scores, GMAC tells schools to "consider that the scores are based on 30-minute, first-draft writing samples. They are not comparable to prepared essays that may be submitted with a school application."

If you score a 4.5 or better (and probably a 4.0 as well), you should not worry about whether somebody on an admissions committee actually reads your handiwork.

How should you think about the AWA essay, as you prepare for the GMAT?

If you are relatively confident that you'll be in the upper 60–80% of test-takers, then you can do minimal preparation:

- **Read the rest of this chapter** and follow the instructions in "How to Prepare for the Essay."
  - **Do GMAT Write.**
  - **Do at least one practice test with the essay.**
- **Go in with a game plan.** Know the structure you're likely to follow.
- **Write a lot.** Longer essays generally score higher.
- **Treat the essay as a warm-up,** saving your energy for the rest of the GMAT.

However, **if you think you're at risk of a score in the bottom 20%, then you need to buckle down**. To judge your risk, ask yourself these questions:

- *Do you have little experience writing academic English?*
  - Did you rarely write essays in English in school?
  - Were your grades in English classes low?
  - In your job, do you rarely write anything longer or more formal than one-line emails?

- *Is your command of written academic English weak?*

  If you're unsure, choose a long Reading Comprehension passage at random and read it with no time pressure, then ask yourself these questions:
    - Are there many words that you didn't understand?
    - Did you fail to understand sentences when they got too long?
    - Did you take 10 minutes or more to finish the passage, only to find that you had little idea what it meant?
    - Did you frequently translate back into another language?

- *Is your command of spoken English weak?*
    - Do you struggle to keep up with a conversation among native English speakers?
    - Do you have a lot more trouble understanding English over the phone than in person?
    - Do you frequently strain to formulate new or complex ideas in English?

If you answer "Yes" to several of these questions, read this chapter carefully, do all the exercises within, and follow the instructions in the last section of this chapter: **"Additional Preparation."**

The Physical Mechanics of Essay Writing

You will be typing your essay into a text box, which takes up part of the screen. You can enter as much text as you want, but you can only see about 10 lines before you have to scroll.

The system feels like a clunky, old-fashioned word-processing program. You have just a few buttons with standard functions:

Button	Function	Keyboard Shortcuts
Cut	Cuts text and puts it on a clipboard.	Ctrl-X or Alt-T
Copy	Copies text onto the clipboard.	Ctrl-C or Alt-C
Paste	Pastes text from the clipboard.	Ctrl-V or Alt-P
Undo	Undoes the last edit you made. You can undo your last 10 edits.	Ctrl-Z or Alt-U
Redo	Redoes something you just undid. You can redo the last 10 undone actions.	Ctrl-Y or Alt-R

Navigation keys on the keyboard act as you expect:

Arrow Keys move the cursor up, down, left, or right.

Enter and **Return** insert a paragraph break and move you to a new line.

Page Up moves the cursor up one screen.

Page Down moves the cursor down one screen.

Backspace removes the character to the left of the cursor.

Delete removes the character to the right of the cursor.

Home moves the cursor to the beginning of the line.

End moves the cursor to the end of the line.

There is no <u>underline</u>, *italic*, or **bold**. Do not use any text-message substitutes (e.g., *asterisks* or ALL CAPS). Rely on the words themselves to convey emphasis.

There is no tab or indent. To start a new paragraph, hit Return a couple of times. This way, you'll put a blank line between paragraphs. If you like to indent the beginning of paragraphs, hit the space bar a small, consistent number of times (say, five).

There is no spell check or grammar check. Good spelling and grammar are better than bad spelling and grammar, of course, so do your best in the moment to avoid mistakes. But don't labor excessively. Follow spelling and grammatical rules well enough to make your meaning clear, but keep writing. On this assignment, more is generally better.

5

What the Argument Essay Specifically Wants

The Argument Essay asks you to analyze an argument—something with a conclusion and premises, as you've learned on Critical Reasoning. In fact, your Critical Reasoning tools will come in handy as you tackle the essay.

The argument that you need to analyze will contain a conclusion, or big claim, along with a few premises. Here's an invented, slightly extreme example:

> The country of Tarquinia has a much higher rate of traffic accidents per person than its neighbors, and in the vast majority of cases one or more drivers is found to be at fault in the courts. Therefore, Tarquinia should abolish driver-side seatbelts, airbags, and other safety measures that protect the driver, while new cars should be installed with a spike on the steering column pointed at the driver's heart. These measures will eliminate traffic accidents in Tarquinia by motivating drivers to drive safely.

Here, the conclusion is that "these measures" (abolishing driver-side safety measures and installing the death spike) "will eliminate traffic accidents in Tarquinia by motivating drivers to drive safely." The premises are listed in the first sentence: the higher rate of traffic accidents and the finding of driver fault. The second sentence describes the proposed measures and can be seen as part of the conclusion.

We'll come back to this gruesome example. Next, you will be given these instructions every time:

> Discuss how well reasoned you find this argument. In your discussion, be sure to analyze the line of reasoning and the use of evidence in the argument. For example, you may need to consider what questionable assumptions underlie the thinking and what alternative explanations or counterexamples might weaken the conclusion. You can also discuss what sort of evidence would strengthen or refute the argument, what changes in the argument would make it more logically sound, and what, if anything, would help you better evaluate its conclusion.

Let's break these four sentences down. The first sentence is the most important:

Sentence 1:   "Discuss **how well reasoned** you find this argument."

This is the core task. Hint: the argument will *never* be very well reasoned! There will always be flaws. Your goal is to find those flaws and explain them clearly.

Sentence 2:   "In your discussion, be sure to analyze the **line of reasoning** and the **use of evidence** in the argument."

The GMAT says you should "be sure to" analyze these two things. So do so!

Line of reasoning
- Does the conclusion follow completely logically from the premises? (No!) Why not?
- What and where are the gaps? Under what circumstances does the logic fail?
- What would you need to prove the conclusion?

Use of evidence
- Does the evidence truly prove what the author wants it to? (No!) Why not?
- What does the given evidence actually prove? Under what circumstances?

Sentence 3:   "For example, you may need to consider what **questionable assumptions** underlie the thinking and what **alternative explanations** or **counterexamples** might weaken the conclusion."

In order to analyze the line of reasoning and use of evidence, you "may need to consider" a few things. Go ahead and consider:

Questionable assumptions
- At each stage of the logic, what has the author assumed that is not necessarily justified?

Alternative explanations or counterexamples
- What else might explain the facts?
- What situations, cases, or circumstances has the author overlooked?

Sentence 4:   "You can also discuss what sort of evidence would strengthen or refute the argument, what changes in the argument would make it more logically sound, and what, if anything, would help you better evaluate its conclusion."

This instruction lists extra aspects that won't hurt your essay and could even help it, but you don't have to include them:

- Possible evidence that would strengthen or weaken the argument
- Possible improvements to the argument
- Possible ways to evaluate the argument

The last items listed in the instructions are worthwhile but *less* important. You can get a 6.0 without paying these aspects too much mind.

Don't forget your fundamental task: **identify and coherently explain the logical flaws in the argument**.

You are not asked to argue *for* or *against* the conclusion. Don't say whether you agree or disagree with it. Rather, analyze the logical strength of the argument: how well the conclusion is supported by the premises. If you find yourself passing judgment on the conclusion itself, recast that judgment as a criticism of the logic. Otherwise, drop the judgment altogether.

Do not bring in excessive outside information. Of course, when you think of counterexamples and so on, you must draw on your knowledge of the world, but only do so in clear service of the analysis.

Again, Chapter 11 in *The Official Guide for GMAT Review, 13th Edition* includes example essays, specifically a 6.0 (Outstanding), a 4.0 (Adequate), and a 2.0 (Seriously Flawed) written for the same prompt. These essays are also included in the *12th edition*, if that's the one you have. Analysis of these essays will be shared over the rest of this chapter; for now, just know that you should read these essays, along with the explanations of how the scores were determined.

The same chapter contains 135 topics that represent nearly every possible essay you'll be asked to write. In fact, if you're hankering for the complete list of 145 possible topics, download it for free from:

www.mba.com/the-gmat/test-structure-and-overview/
analytical-writing-assessment-section.aspx

The specific link is as follows, though it may change:

www.mba.com/the-gmat/test-structure-and-overview/~/media/Files/mba/
NEWTheGMAT/AnalysisofanArgument100606.ashx

The 10 additional topics in the online list are very similar to other 135 topics published in the *Official Guide*.

What should you do with all these topics? Practically nothing if you fall in the top 60–80%. Do not indulge any perfectionist whim ("I know how to ace the essay task! I'll write 145 essays ahead of time and memorize them, so I can spit them back out on test day!") This use of your time is quite possibly the worst you can imagine. If you really want to, go ahead and glance at the topics, but do nothing else.

However, if you need extra preparation for the AWA (because your score is or is likely to be low), you'll use these sample topics to write practice essays. We'll describe this activity at the end of the chapter.

How to Structure the Task

To write a decent essay in only 30 minutes, you need a clear process, such as this one:

1.   Read (1–2 min)
2.   Brainstorm (2 min)
3.   Outline (1–2 min)
4.   Write (20 min)
5.   Polish (3–5 min)

Step 1. Read (1–2 min)

First, clear your mind and read the argument slowly and carefully. Don't race through the reading. Thirty minutes is not very long, but take a minute or even two to absorb the argument as written. If you don't take your time, you may overlook opportunities for your essay.

As you read, identify the conclusion—the big claim that the author is making. The rest of the argument typically consists of background information and premises—facts and smaller claims made to support the conclusion. This support will always be flawed in some way. You will not be asked to analyze a completely airtight argument.

Step 2. Brainstorm (2 min)

See below for "How to Generate Good Ideas." Jot your ideas on the scratchpad or type them directly into the computer. Either way, don't write too much at this point—just enough to remind you of your thoughts.

Step 3. Outline (1–2 min)

See below for "How to Structure the Essay." Put a short placeholder into the text box for each point.

Step 4. Write (20 min)

Now go to town. Volume matters. The three scored examples in the *Official Guide* show a clear pattern:

Score	Word Count
6.0	335
4.0	260
2.0	108

The example of a 6.0 on mba.com (an essay that was actually written by a test-taker) has 599 words! There's no need to write that much; aim for around 300 words.

Adding volume is not simply a matter of writing more words. You should also strive to lengthen your sentences appropriately, as the examples demonstrate.

Score	Word Count	Sentences	Words per Sentence
6.0	335	13	25.8
6.0 (mba.com)	599	26	23.0
4.0	260	15	17.3
2.0	108	8	13.5

Aim for around 20 words a sentence, not as a strict measure to apply in every case, but rather as a rough average. Write 15 sentences averaging 20 words per sentence, and you'll have 300 words.

Of course, the real trick is to make your prose worth reading. How do you not only lengthen your sentences but improve them? See below for "How to Write Better Sentences."

Step 5. Polish — a Little (3–5 min)

With a few minutes to go, turn off the spigot. Glance back over what you've written and smooth out the worst of the rough edges. Don't take too much time on any one sentence, gnawing your pencil to find the *mot juste* (the "perfect word" in French). Don't try to write French. Don't try to be Shakespeare.

To switch to a homely metaphor, just splash some cologne on the oinking pig of your essay, pat its hair down, and push it out the door. Let your not-so-beautiful creation go find its destiny. Clear your mind to take on the rest of the GMAT.

In fact, if you're confident about the essay, you might want to finish half a minute or so early. You don't get a break before Integrated Reasoning, but you can make your own mini-break by finishing your essay slightly early and then waiting to hit Submit. Don't worry—if you somehow don't actually hit the button, what you've written will still be submitted.

During your self-made break, you won't be able to get up and walk around, but take a few deep breaths, roll your shoulders, and massage your neck. The extra seconds you take to manage your bodily state will do you good going into IR, which you will probably find more challenging.

How to Generate Good Ideas

For your essay, you need a few ideas about flaws in the argument. You need more than one idea, but you don't need multitudes.

The key to brainstorming is to follow a method, four of which are described below. Read about them all, then take your pick. Whatever seems most comfortable now is what's going to work best.

Whichever method you use, jot down just enough to capture the idea. Don't write too much. Then look for another idea. Here's how: imagine that the flaw that you just spotted is now fixed. What *else* is wrong with the argument? Once you've identified 3–4 flaws, move to the Outline phase.

Brainstorming Method 1: Line by Line

Start with the first sentence in the argument. What's wrong with it?
- If it's a piece of evidence, how does it fail to prove the bigger point?
- If it's a claim, how is it not supported by the evidence?

Work your way, sentence by sentence, to the end of the argument.

Brainstorming Method 2: The CAST System

CAST is an acronym to remind you what you're looking for:

Counterexamples
- What situations would disprove the author's assertions?

Assumptions
- What is the author assuming, probably in an unjustified way?

Strengthen
- What would strengthen the argument?

Terms
- What specific words in the argument create logical gaps or other problems?

Go letter by letter through CAST and jot down ideas.

Brainstorming Method 3: Use the Instructions

You'll always be provided with the same instructions, so you can use them as a checklist. The first sentence gives you the core task. The second sentence reminds you what to look *at*:

- Line of reasoning
- Use of evidence

The third sentence reminds you what to look *for*:

- Questionable assumptions
- Alternative explanations or counterexamples

Finally, the fourth sentence reminds you about other stuff you can add to your essay.

Brainstorming Method 4: Remember Common Fallacies

In the sample essay prompts (and in Critical Reasoning arguments, for that matter), many of the same logical fallacies show up again and again. If you have trouble spotting flaws, review a list of these fallacies. We have an extended list in our *Foundations of GMAT Verbal* book. Here's a condensed list with a few alterations:

1. **Alternative Causes**
   If the author asserts that X causes Y, what *else* could be the cause of Y?
   Correlation ≠ Causation: If X and Y happen at the same time, it's not necessarily true that X causes Y. It could be that Y causes X, or some Z causes them both, or they just randomly happen together on this one occasion.
   After ≠ Because: If Y happens *after* X, it's not necessarily true that Y happens *because of* X. Some other cause could be at work.
   Future ≠ Past: If X did cause Y in the past, will X always cause Y in the future? Not necessarily. Circumstances could change.

2. **Unforeseen Consequences**
   If the author proposes Plan A to achieve Goal B, what could go *wrong*?
   Nothing's Perfect: How could the plan fail to achieve the stated goal? Does it go too far or not far enough? What implementation challenges has the author overlooked?
   Isn't It Ironic: What bad side effects of the plan could happen? These side effects might be bad on their own, or they might directly prevent the plan from achieving its goal. Economic examples of the latter include customer attrition (if you raise prices to increase revenue, customers may flee) and price wars (if you cut your price to gain market share, your competition could cut prices in response). Think about who has been ignored by the author (such as customers and competitors) and what their negative responses to the plan might be.
   Skill & Will: If people are involved in implementing the plan (and they always are), you need the people to have both the *skill* to succeed and the *will* to succeed. Do they? Who benefits from the plan, and are they the same people who need to carry it out?

3. **Faulty Use of Evidence**
   What is sketchy about the evidence—not factually, but how the author uses it?
   Limited Sample: Do you have too little data? How are the mentioned cases not representative of the wider world?

Troubled Analogy: If the author draws a conclusion about M from facts about "similar" N, how are M and N different? What differing conditions has the author ignored? *What It Really Means:* The evidence simply may not imply what the author claims that it does.

4.   **Faulty Use of Language**
      What *Extreme* words does the author use? What *Vague* terms are in the argument? Have any terms been *Switched*? You may even encounter a math fallacy, such as *Percents vs. Real Quantities*.

Now that you have plenty of ideas about possible flaws (and how to brainstorm them), let's look at the flaws described in an example essay: the 6.0 essay in *The Official Guide for GMAT Review, 13th Edition* (or *12th Edition*). The given argument proposes an automatic early warning system to eliminate midair collisions between airplanes. Four flaws in this argument are pointed out in the second paragraph of the essay. Here's a brief list, as if they were brainstormed:

- • Assumes cause of collisions = lack of knowledge
  - – What if pilots don't pay attention to the warning system?
- • Assumes pilots automatically obey the warning
  - – What if they don't?
- • Limited to commercial planes
  - – What about other kinds of planes?
- • What if the system fails?

The first two flaws are examples of the *Skill & Will* fallacy. The last two flaws are examples of *Nothing's Perfect:* the plan doesn't go far enough, and it ignores the possibility of failure.

Not every flaw in the argument is captured in the essay. That's fine! For instance, the author never criticizes the use of the extreme word "eliminate" in the conclusion ("reduce" would be more defensible). The point is that you can get a 6.0 on the essay without considering every last flaw in the argument.

Go ahead and brainstorm flaws in the Tarquinia argument. Take 2 minutes and use any method you prefer in order to generate 3–5 specific flaws. Here is the prompt again; cover up the answers below the box.

> The country of Tarquinia has a much higher rate of traffic accidents per person than its neighbors, and in the vast majority of cases one or more drivers is found to be at fault in the courts. Therefore, Tarquinia should abolish driver-side seatbelts, airbags, and other safety measures that protect the driver, while new cars should be installed with a spike on the steering column pointed at the driver's heart. These measures will eliminate traffic accidents in Tarquinia by motivating drivers to drive safely.

Now compare your results to this sample list:

• Higher accident rate = meaningful?
   – What if Tarquinia is not comparable to its neighbors?
     (car ownership, rural/urban mix might be different)
	Troubled Analogy

• Guilt in courts = true guilt? – What if courts are bad or just bureaucratic? Ignores other factors.	*What It Really Means*

• Extreme punishment (fender bender = death)
   – Who will support, implement?
   – People would disable the system.
	Skill & Will

• Only applies to new cars – System only works if *all* cars are deadly to drivers.	*Nothing's Perfect*
• Who would buy new cars? No one!	*Isn't It Ironic*

On first reading the argument, you may have felt that the proposed measures were extreme. However, you aren't supposed to talk about whether *you* yourself agree with the argument.

The way to work this negative reaction of yours into the list of flaws is to imagine how other people might react similarly. Most reasonable folks would consider this proposal extreme, and so it would be nearly impossible to get car manufacturers, dealers, and the rest of the population to stick to the plan. Recast your own judgments as logical flaws in the argument itself. If the argument involves a plan, your negative reaction probably indicates a serious implementation challenge.

How to Structure the Essay

The simple structure you should use has three parts:

1. Introduction
2. Body
3. Conclusion

How you structure the body and the conclusion can vary, but the intro can always work the same way.

Introduction

1. Restate the argument *briefly*:

> "The author proposes plan X to accomplish goal Y...."

2. Make a single "controlling point" or broad statement about how the argument fails to work in general.

For example, the controlling point of the 6.0 example essay in the *Official Guide* is spread across a couple of sentences:

> "The statement... simply describes the [warning] system.... This alone does not consti-
> tute a logical argument... and it certainly does not provide support or proof...."

Notice how general this controlling point is! The essay writer is saying in a fancy way that the argument doesn't work. That's all you have to do. For example:

> "This plan is fundamentally flawed, in that...

> > "... the evidence provided fails to support the author's claim...."
> > *or*
> > "... the argument is riddled with serious logical gaps...."
> > *or*
> > "... the argument makes numerous unwarranted assumptions...."

You don't have to preview all the specific flaws here in the intro. In fact, you probably shouldn't.

If you'd like to give a positive nod to the argument, do so *before* your controlling point using a "conces-
sion" word such as *although*:

> "Although the argument has some merits, a number of defects undermine the claim...."

Body

1. Describe and justify 3–5 specific flaws in the argument. That's the purpose of the body. If you brainstormed more than five flaws, pick the best and drop the rest.

You can put all the flaws in one big paragraph, as the 6.0 example essay does. Describe each flaw in one sentence, then justify it in another:

- "One basic flaw in the argument is…."
- "But what if…?" (counterexample)
- "The proposal also fails to consider…."
- "As a result, implementation would become…." (implication)

In this case, save your discussion of improvements for the conclusion.

Alternatively, you can put each flaw in a separate body paragraph if you have a lot to say about each one. If you split the body into more than one paragraph, then go ahead and talk about how you would fix the flaws, so that you avoid very short paragraphs. You should average 3–5 sentences per paragraph.

You can even group a couple of flaws together in one paragraph, if they are related. For instance, you could make one body paragraph about *poor use of evidence* (with 2–3 flaws) and another about *faulty line of reasoning* (with another 2–3 flaws).

Conclusion

1. Recap *briefly* how the argument is flawed:

"In summary…."

2. Mention fixes to the argument if you haven't already:

"To address the problems in the argument, one would have to… (gather more data of XYZ kind) (run pilot projects to test the hypothesis) (etc.)"

Use new language in your recap. You're saying, yet again, that the argument is flawed, but you need a novel way to say it. Replace particular words (e.g., "flaw") with synonyms ("error, gap, mistake, defect, fault, imperfection").

If you haven't already discussed possible improvements, do so here. If you are searching for still other things to say—and you have time—revisit the last sentence of the instructions. You can discuss possible new evidence or ways to evaluate the argument. Note that the 6.0 essay published in the *Official Guide* gives *very* short shrift to potential improvements. All the essay really does is explain the flaws; only the very last sentence gives a nod to fixes.

By the way, avoid humor in general. Play this particular game pretty straight. That said, don't be afraid to let your personality shine through, if that helps you generate the volume of content you need.

How to Write Better Sentences

You can become a better writer if you focus on improving the actual sentences you write. No matter how you feel about the essay, why not learn how to make your sentences better in general? For one thing, your efforts will pay off on the rest of the GMAT: the more you understand about sentence construction, the better *reader* you'll be on test day. And every part of the GMAT demands that you read sentences quickly and effectively.

By the way, if you're a non-native speaker, GMAC says that "in considering the elements of standard written English, readers are trained to be sensitive and fair in evaluating the responses of examinees whose first language is not English." In other words, you'll get a little consideration. How much? Probably not tons. The good news is that if you've learned English as a second language, you're conscious of the grammatical issues that can empower you to write better sentences.

Structure Your Sentences — Then Flesh Them Out

A sentence should represent a thought. Thus, the core structure of the sentence should represent the skeleton of that thought, stripped of all flesh.

To analyze a sentence quickly, break it into Topic and Comment:

> Topic: what you're talking about
> Comment: what you're saying about the Topic

Take the first sentence in the 6.0 example essay in the *Official Guide*. Strip that sentence down to its essentials to find the Topic-Comment structure:

The argument…	omits concerns.
Topic	*Comment*
"What are you talking about?"	"What are you saying about that argument?"

At the simplest level, the Topic is often the bare grammatical subject, while the Comment is the simple predicate (that is, a verb and maybe an object).

The argument…	omits…	concerns.
Subject	*Verb*	*Object*
"What is doing the action?"	"What action?"	"To what?"

Good sentences have obvious — and intentional — core structures.

Now, how do you expand upon the core? How do you put flesh on the bones? You have many options.

1. Make compounds with *and, or,* and the like.

You can make compounds of individual words, such as nouns and verbs:

> The argument omits or *downplays* concerns.
> The argument omits *both concerns and criticisms.*

You can also make compounds at the sentence level:

> The argument omits concerns, *and it downplays criticisms.*

Use this latter construction sparingly as a device to lengthen your sentences. Rely more on the next two tools.

2. Add modifiers to describe parts of the sentence.

As you probably know from your preparation for Sentence Correction, the simplest modifiers are single words (adjectives, adverbs, and possessives):

> *Single words:* The *author's* argument *completely* omits *valid* concerns.

Modifiers answer questions about parts of the sentence: *Whose* argument? *What kinds* of concerns? *To what degree* does the argument omit concerns?

Modifiers can consist of several words. Whereas single-word modifiers often come before the thing they're modifying, multi-word modifiers almost always come afterwards:

> *Phrases:* The argument *of the author* omits concerns *about implementation.*
> *Clauses:* The argument *that the author makes* omits concerns *that must be addressed.*

Clauses contain working verbs (*makes, must be addressed*) and sometimes subjects as well (*the author*).

You can embed modifiers within other modifiers. The full first sentence of the 6.0 essay is nothing but a single Subject–Verb–Object core with modifier attachments. Here is that sentence in all its poetic glory:

The argument
    that   *Which argument? The argument that...*
        this
            warning   *What kind of system? This warning system.*
    system
    will
        virtually   *To what degree will the system solve the problem? Virtually.*
    solve
    the problem
        of   *Which problem? The problem of collisions.*
            midair plane   *What kind of collisions? Midair plane collisions.*
        collisions
omits
    some important   *What kinds of concerns? Some important ones.*
concerns
    that   *What kinds of concerns? Ones that must be addressed.*
        must be addressed
        to   *For what purpose must they be addressed? To substantiate....*
            substantiate
            the argument.

5

These modifiers take the sentence from 4 words to 27! Remember that you're aiming for an average of 20–25 words per sentence. Modifiers are a great way to lengthen and enrich sentences. To add modifiers, ask questions of the parts you already have in place: Which argument? What kinds of concerns? How, why, to what degree, for what purpose?

3. Add sentence-level subordinate clauses.

Words such as *because*, *since*, *if*, and *although* indicate logical connections between your thoughts, acting like tendons between muscles and bones:

> The argument omits concerns, *although it has merits.*

You should often put concessions first, so that you can pack a punch with your subsequent assertion—and then follow up with evidence:

> *Although the argument has merits*, it omits concerns. For instance....

You can also use a semicolon to join two sentences, adding a relational word such as *therefore* or *moreover*. The part after the semicolon is not a subordinate clause, technically, but the logical relationship between the two original sentences is tighter than if you used a simple *and* as the link:

> The argument omits concerns; *moreover, it downplays criticisms.*

As you use all these tools, experimenting with lengthening sentences, you might find yourself going too far. Avoid prose obesity. Keep your sentences trim, and make every word count. To avoid putting your readers to sleep, vary the structure and length of your sentences.

If you have a cumbersome sentence, first try breaking it into more than one sentence. If that doesn't work, move the heavy stuff to the end. Shift the grammatical core up front, so that a reader doesn't have to wade through a whole lot of modifiers to understand the gist of what the sentence is saying.

Pay Attention to Grammar (to a Degree)

You need to know grammatical rules for Sentence Correction; you might as well apply this knowledge to sentence *construction*, too. Yes, you can make occasional mistakes with grammar in your writing, as noted earlier. After all, the AWA rewards volume. If you have a choice between writing a new sentence and polishing another sentence's grammar, you should generally write the new sentence!

All that said, the better your grammar, the clearer your thoughts. Pay attention to the following issues.

Parallelism: When you use parallel markers such as and, make the parts logically and structurally parallel:

    X and Y   X, Y, and Z   both X and Y   X or Y   not only X but also Y

Pronouns: Remember the Deadly Five—*it, its, they, them,* and *their*? In your writing, try to ensure that these words have clear, meaningful antecedents—the nouns that they refer to. Sloppy pronoun reference reveals sloppy thinking. For example:

Sloppy: If cars go too fast on the highway, it can cause crashes.

What does *it* refer to? The highway?

Better: If cars go too fast on the highway, crashes can occur.
Cars that go too fast on the highway can cause crashes.
Highway speeding can cause crashes.

Modifiers: Put modifiers next to the thing you want to modify.

Your essay does not have to exhibit perfect grammar to get a great score, let alone a decent score. Even 6.0 essays can have minor grammatical flaws, even a series of them, as you'll see below.

By the way, feel free to use the passive voice. For one thing, it's grammatically correct. More importantly, the passive voice in English provides a useful way of flipping sentences around, so that you can control the Topic-Comment structure as you desire.

Highway speeding…	can cause crashes.
Topic	*Comment*
"What are you talking about?"	"What are you saying about ***highway speeding***?"

Crashes...	can be caused by highway speeding.
Topic	*Comment*
"What are you talking about?"	"What are you saying about **crashes**?"

Choose Your Words — and Vary Them

Words are like notes on a piano. Play them and play around with them to appreciate their resonance. For the AWA essay, it's worth distinguishing two categories of words: *signal words* and *substance words*.

Signal words indicate relationships to previous text. Signals are super-handy as you *read* academic text (for instance, passages in Reading Comprehension). The same words are also super-handy as you *write* that kind of text. For this reason, we've reprinted below the list of signal words from chapter 1 of our *Reading Comprehension Strategy Guide*. Use these words liberally in your essay. Don't be afraid of telling your readers exactly where they are and what's happening. Be an over-enthusiastic tour guide of your thinking.

Relationship	**Signal**
Focus attention	As for, Regarding, In reference to
Add to previous point	Furthermore, Moreover, In addition, As well as, Also, Likewise, Too
Provide contrast	On one hand / On the other hand, While, Rather, Instead, In contrast, Alternatively
Provide conceding contrast (author unwillingly agrees)	Granted, It is true that, Certainly, Admittedly, Despite, Although
Provide emphatic contrast (author asserts own position)	But, However, Even so, All the same, Still, That said, Nevertheless, Nonetheless, Yet, Otherwise, Despite [concession], [assertion]
Dismiss previous point	In any event, In any case
Point out similarity	Likewise, In the same way
Structure the discussion	First, Second, etc., To begin with, Next, Finally, Again
Give example	For example, In particular, For instance
Generalize	In general, To a great extent, Broadly speaking
Sum up, perhaps with exception	In conclusion, In brief, Overall, Except for, Besides
Indicate logical result	Therefore, Thus, As a result, So, Accordingly, Hence
Indicate logical cause	Because, Since, As, Resulting from
Restate for clarity	In other words, That is, Namely, So to speak
Hedge or soften position	Apparently, At least, Can, Could, May, Might, Should, Possibly, Likely
Strengthen position	After all, Must, Have to, Always, Never, etc.

| Introduce surprise | Actually, In fact, Indeed |
| Reveal author's attitude | Fortunately, Unfortunately, *other adverbs*, So-called |

Substance words contain real content. Our main suggestion here is to have a mini-thesaurus up your sleeve for certain ideas that you are likely to express—and re-express—*no matter what particular essay you must write*. For instance, you will need to have more than one way of making this point:

"The argument is flawed."

Simply memorizing any list of synonyms and spitting them back out will do you little good. The 2.0 ("Seriously Flawed") essay published in the *Official Guide* is riddled with these terms, seemingly as a substitute for thought. But you don't want to spend a lot of time searching for another way to say that an argument is *flawed*. Use these lists to free your mind up to do real thinking:

| *Argument is good:* | sound, persuasive, thorough, convincing, logical, compelling, credible, effective |
| *perfect:* | airtight, watertight |

Argument is bad:	flawed (of course!), defective, imperfect, faulty, fallacious, unpersuasive, unconvincing, ineffective; it over-generalizes, makes an extreme claim, takes a logical leap, makes an unwarranted assumption, fails to justify X or prove Y or address Z
really bad:	unsound, illogical, specious, erroneous, invalid, unfounded, baseless
maliciously bad:	misleading, deceptive

| *Flaw:* | defect, omission, fault, error, failing, imperfection; concern, issue, area, aspect, feature to be addressed, opportunity for improvement |

| *Assess an argument:* | judge, evaluate, critique, examine, scrutinize, weigh |

| *Strengthen an argument:* | support, bolster, substantiate, reinforce, improve, fortify, justify, address concerns, fix issues, reduce or eliminate defects; prove (a very high standard) |
| *Weaken an argument:* | undermine, damage, harm, water down, impair, remove support for; disprove (also a high standard), destroy, demolish, annihilate, obliterate |

Practice swapping words in your emails. Use Shift-F7 (PC) or the Dictionary (Mac) to call up a thesaurus and avail yourself of the *treasury* of English words (that's what *thesaurus* means). Don't go too wild—no word is precisely interchangeable with any other. If an entry in the thesaurus is an attractive but mysterious stranger, call up the dictionary and confirm the core meaning of the word. Then dig up examples of reputable use in print, so that you learn the word's strength, spin, and tonal qualities.

In your essay, avoid slang and jargon. You risk confusing or even offending your readers. You don't have to stick to highly formal registers of English; feel free to use contractions (such as *don't*) and short, concrete words (such as *stick to*). However, only write what's appropriate for an academic paper.

Sentence-by-Sentence Analysis of the 6.0 Essay

Let's examine each sentence in the 6.0 example essay in the *Official Guide*:

Paragraph 1, Sentence 1

The argument...	omits...	concerns
Subject	*Verb*	*Object*

To the core S–V–O structure, various modifiers are added, as you've already seen.

Paragraph 1, Sentence 2

The statement...	describes...	the system and [how it operates]
Subject	*Verb*	*Object*

The object is compound: *X and Y*. The second part of the object is known as a noun clause: a mini-sentence (*it operates*) with a word (*how*) that allows the whole thing to act like a noun in a bigger sentence. Instead, the author could have written an action noun: *its operation*. Either way is good enough. The noun clause *how it operates* is perhaps not as parallel to *the system* as you'd like, but the GMAT won't care about this minor degree of parallelism violation on the AWA.

Various modifiers are added, including an adverb (*simply*) and a subordinate clause (*that follows...*) that happens to contain another noun clause (*what this warning system will do*).

Paragraph 1, Sentence 3

This...	does not constitute...	an argument..., and	it...	does not provide...	support or proof
Subject	*Verb*	*Object*	*Subject*	*Verb*	*Object*

This sentence is compound: *full sentence, and full sentence*. The second object is compound (*or*). The word *This* without a noun following does not have a completely clear antecedent (the author seems to mean *the statement*, the subject of the prior sentence). Again, the AWA scorers are willing to accept minor grammatical blemishes of this kind. The compound core is fleshed out by a variety of modifiers.

Paragraph 2, Sentence 1

The argument…	does not address…	the cause…, the use…, or [who is involved…]
Subject	*Verb*	*Object*

The object is triply compound: *X*, *Y*, or *Z*. The third part is another noun clause—again, not as parallel as would be ideal, but remember that this essay got the top score.

An adverb is placed as a signal word at the start of the sentence: *Most conspicuously*. In that position, the adverb comments on the entire thought.

Paragraph 2, Sentence 2

The argument	assumes	that…
Subject	*Verb*	*Object*

the cause	is	that…
Subject	*Verb*	*Object*

X, Y, and Z	are	A or B
Subject	*Verb*	*Adjectives*

This sentence looks more complicated than it is. After a verb, what the word *that* does is allow you to embed a whole sentence as the object of the verb:

"My mother believes *that I am right*."

What does my mother believe? She believes something: *that I am right*.

Having two levels (one outer and one inner) is totally fine. Three pushes the limit, as in the case above. Never go four levels deep: *My mother believes that the argument assumes that the cause is that…*. As in the movie *Inception*, at that depth you just might lose your grip on reality.

The most embedded level in the sentence has a triply-compound subject, connected by a linking verb (*are*) to two adjectives. Modifiers are sprinkled throughout (e.g., the signal word *First*).

This sentence loses its thread somewhat; it goes too deep and tries to pack too much in. Once again, remember that this essay earned a 6.0. You can get away with a few clunkers.

Paragraph 2, Sentence 3

The argument…	describes…	a system
Subject	*Verb*	*Object*

A variation that's new to this sentence is an opening modifier: *In a weak attempt to support its claim.* Occasionally throw in such a modifier, rather than lead with a bare subject or a simple signal word or phrase.

Paragraph 2, Sentence 4

But if	the cause...	is	that...
	Subject	*Verb*	*Object*

	pilots	are not paying	attention... ,
	Subject	*Verb*	*Object*

system...	will not solve	the problem
Subject	*Verb*	*Object*

We're now encountering a sentence-level subordinate clause: *If [subordinate clause], main sentence.* The subordinate clause has one level of Inception-style embedding: *the cause is that....*

The signal word *But* indicates a clear contrast to what's come before.

Paragraph 2, Sentence 5

The argument...	never addresses...	the interface... and [how this will affect...]
Subject	*Verb*	*Object*

The author continues to earn minor traffic violations: the two parts of the object are not as parallel as the GMAT would want in Sentence Correction, and the additional floating *this* could raise a grammarian's eyebrows. Your takeaway should be that your grammar need not be perfect on this essay. What's more important is the quality (and quantity) of your thinking.

The signal word *Second* broadcasts our position in the list of flaws.

Paragraph 2, Sentence 6

If	the pilot or flight specialist...	does not conform...
	Subject	*Verb*

collisions...	will not be avoided
Subject	*Verb*

The second verb is in the passive voice, a completely appropriate choice.

Paragraph 2, Sentence 7

If   planes...   are involved...
     Subject   *Verb*

the problem...   cannot be solved...   by a system...
Subject   *Verb*   *Agent*

> The passive voice is again used in the main clause. This time, the agent is indicated in the phrase *by a system*. The signal word *Finally* indicates that the list of flaws is wrapping up.

Paragraph 2, Sentence 8

The argument...   does not address...   [what would happen in the event that...]
Subject   *Verb*   *Object*

> The object is another noun clause (a form that the author evidently loves) with an embedded sentence inside (*the warning system collapses...*). The author sneaks another flaw into the essay under the banner of the word *also*. In other words, Finally wasn't final, but this contradiction is negligible in the scheme of things.

Paragraph 3, Sentence 1

Because   the argument...   leaves out...   issues...
     Subject   *Verb*   *Object*

it...   is not...   sound or persuasive
Subject   *Verb*   *Adjectives*

> Some folks believe that you cannot start a sentence with *Because*. You can, as long as you follow the *Because* clause with a main clause, as the author does correctly here. The word *it* has a clear antecedent (*the argument*).

Paragraph 3, Sentence 2

If   it...   included...   the items...
     Subject   *Verb*   *Object*

the argument...   would have been...   more thorough and convincing
Subject   *Verb*   *Adjectives*

> The pronoun *it* still clearly refers to *the argument* from the previous sentence.

Technically, the two clauses don't match in tense. Grammarians would say that you can write *If it included… it would be…* OR *If it had included… it would have been….* Evidently, the AWA graders didn't care, in the end.

Sample Essay

Had enough sentence analysis? Itching to get on with it and *write*?

Here's the Tarquinia essay again. On your computer, open up a basic word processor (WordPad or NotePad), one that doesn't have any spelling or grammar check. Alternatively, open up Word and disable automatic spell/grammar check.

Set a timer for 30 minutes, and go to town.

> The country of Tarquinia has a much higher rate of traffic accidents per person than its neighbors, and in the vast majority of cases one or more drivers is found to be at fault in the courts. Therefore, Tarquinia should abolish driver-side seatbelts, airbags, and other safety measures that protect the driver, while new cars should be installed with a spike on the steering column pointed at the driver's heart. These measures will eliminate traffic accidents in Tarquinia by motivating drivers to drive safely.

> Discuss how well reasoned you find this argument. In your discussion, be sure to analyze the line of reasoning and the use of evidence in the argument. For example, you may need to consider what questionable assumptions underlie the thinking and what alternative explanations or counterexamples might weaken the conclusion. You can also discuss what sort of evidence would strengthen or refute the argument, what changes in the argument would make it more logically sound, and what, if anything, would help you better evaluate its conclusion.

When you're done, cut and paste the results into Microsoft Word, so that you can do a word count. Recall that you're aiming for 300 words and about 15 sentences, for an average of 20 or so words per sentence. If your essay has substantially less than 300 words or 20 words per sentence, you'll need to bulk up.

Next, run the Spelling & Grammar checker. Note any errors, but don't correct them yet. When the program has finished, it will give you a read-out of a couple of useful metrics: Flesch Reading Ease and Flesch-Kincaid Grade Level. These scales, which depend on words per sentence and syllables per word, are crude measures of reading difficulty, but check out the correlation with AWA scores in four published essays.

Source	Score	Words	Sentences	Words/ Sentence	Flesch Reading Ease	Flesch-Kincaid Grade Level
OG	6	335	13	25.8	42.7	13.6
mba.com	6	599	26	23.0	40.5	13.1
OG	4	260	15	17.3	67.5	8.1
OG	2	108	8	13.5	62.3	7.9
Correlation with score	**0.85**	**0.71**	**0.97**	**−0.83**	**0.91**

Here's how correlation works, lest you've forgotten: the closer the number is to 1, the stronger the positive relationship between the two trends. So, for instance, a correlation of 0.97 indicates that for this (admittedly minuscule) sample of essays, the score and the number of words per sentence are almost perfectly correlated. The more words in a sentence, the higher the score.

Remember, though, that correlation does not equal causation! We're not saying that if you just pack more words in each sentence, you'll get a higher score. Rather, better writing is the cause of both effects (higher scores and more words per sentence).

The closer a correlation is to −1, the stronger the negative relationship. So *lower* Flesch Reading Ease scales correlate with higher scores, according to this limited set of data.

The sample is tiny but indicative. Compare your Reading Ease and Grade Level scores to this table to get a sense of how your essay stacks up. Obviously, you can game this system by writing nonsense.

Now take a look at our sample version:

In response to the comparatively high rate of traffic accidents in Tarquinia, as well as to the results of court cases, the author argues that measures should be taken to compromise driver safety, in order to motivate safer driving. This argument suffers from a number of flaws, ranging from flimsy use of evidence to ill conceived elements of the proposal, that would collectively mandate a full re-conception before the proposal could be carried out.

First of all, the author cites two pieces of supporting evidence, which, even if true, should be challenged on the basis of their applicability. Tarquinia may have a higher rate of accidents than its neighbors, but what if those neighbors have vastly different circumstances? Rates of car ownership, highway safety conditions (even including weather), and urban/rural divides would need to be controlled for before reliable conclusions could be drawn. Likewise, it may be true that Tarquinian courts find one or more drivers guilty in most cases, but the degree to which these findings are driven by administrative necessity or other unrelated factors is unknown. Perhaps insurance law in the country demands that one or the other driver be found at fault, even if road conditions are largely to blame. These questions call the utility of the mentioned evidence into question.

Secondly, the design of the plan is highly questionable from the standpoint of practicality, even without consideration of the moral implications. The first accidental fender bender that kills both drivers would cause the population of Tarquinia to reject the proposal as sadistic and extreme. Moreover, the fact that the proposal only applies to new cars creates another logical hole big enough to drive a truck through. No car buyer would purchase a new car willingly, and if any new cars did wind up on the road, the presence of old cars (which would not be subject to driver hazard) would undermine the self-enforcement regime, since not all drivers would be subject to the penalty of death by impalement for poor driving.

It is hard to conceive how this proposal could be fixed. Applying the plan to all cars in Tarquinia raises significant further implementation challenges.

Here are the numbers on this essay:

Words	Sentences	Words/ Sentence	Flesch Reading Ease	Flesch-Kincaid Grade Level
359	14	25.6	40.5	13.9

Go line by line and compare how you expressed a point with how we expressed a similar point. Borrow or steal whatever you find useful—word choices, phrasing, sentence or paragraph structure. How? Simply retype the words or sentences in question. By running them through your fingers, you start to make them your own.

While this essay is not perfect, it's likely good enough to get a 4.5 or higher. That's all you need.

How to Prepare for the Essay

Now that you've gotten this far, do two more things to get ready:

1. Do GMAT Write.

GMAT Write is the gold standard, made by the makers of the GMAT itself. You practice with real prompts and are scored by the same computer algorithm as that used on the real exam.

As of spring 2012, GMAT Write costs $30 on mba.com. If you are a Manhattan GMAT course student, you get a free coupon in your Student Center.

If your score comes back as a 4.5 or higher, rest easy. You just need to take one more step (#2 below). If your score comes back as a 3.5 or lower, see "Additional Preparation" below. Finally, if you get a 4.0, you're on the cusp. You might want to put more time into preparation, but you might be able to skate by without it.

2. Regardless of how GMAT Write went, do at least one practice exam with the essay.

The reason is that you need to build stamina for the whole exam. In particular, by the time you hit the Verbal section, you'll feel "in your legs" the extra half-hour that you spent up front, unless you have been practicing with the essay.

You don't have to do every practice exam this way. In fact, most people shouldn't. But you should definitely do at least one practice exam "as if"—as if it were the real GMAT, all the way through. As sports coaches will tell you, you should practice as you're going to play.

Additional Preparation

If you have scored a 3.5 or lower on GMAT Write or on the real AWA—or you think you will—you need to put more time into preparing for the essay. It's just the way things are. Don't let this essay exercise get in the way of your broader ambitions.

Here are practical steps to take:

1. Work through our *Foundations of GMAT Verbal* book.

You may already be spending time with that book. Great—now you have another reason to focus. *Foundations of GMAT Verbal* covers all three Verbal question types (Sentence Correction, Critical Reasoning, and Reading Comprehension), all of which come into play on the AWA essay. You need the parts of speech and other grammatical principles to tear apart and strengthen the sentences you write. You need to spot missing assumptions and analyze other logical flaws to write an effective essay about a flawed argument. Finally, the better you *read* this kind of text (as in a Reading Comp passage), the better you can *write* this kind of text.

So kill a few birds with one stone. Focus on Verbal basics to build skill for the essay.

2. Rewrite or retype the 6.0 essay in the *Official Guide.*

An underappreciated but effective technique for improving your writing is to copy out the work you're trying to imitate. After all, to learn to *speak* a language, you don't just *listen* to someone speaking. You parrot back what that person says. You give canned responses. After a while, you're experimenting, you're making some choices on the fly, you're stringing together pre-made "chunks." As you go, you're achieving greater and greater fluency. This is how you learn to speak; you can learn to write in a particular style the same way.

3. Read, recopy, and rewrite high-quality articles in English.

Find good source material. Use the *Economist,* the *Smithsonian,* the *Atlantic,* the *New Yorker.* For daily newspapers, hit the *New York Times,* the *Wall Street Journal,* the *Washington Post,* and the *Financial Times.* Go get *Scientific American,* the *Journal of American History,* the *Harvard Business Review,* or the *McKinsey Quarterly.* Pick up an alumni magazine of a top university. Visit aldaily.com for links to wonderful "Arts and Letters" pieces from across the web.

It's good simply to read articles from these sources, as a way of improving your comprehension and your general level of knowledge. Read articles aloud, savoring the words and imbuing them with emphasis and emotion. To really crank up your writing chops, though, you must pass some of the words through your pen.

You can take notes of individual words, adding them to a vocabulary list. That's well and good. Much more importantly, you need to internalize the bigger picture—the way words are strung into phrases and clauses, which then lock together into sentences, which then are crafted into paragraphs. One way to do this is to force yourself to play all the notes, so to speak. How? Recopy them one by one.

If you get really ambitious, you can *rewrite* a piece, summarizing it or playing with language in some other way. But even if you just recopy the words verbatim, you'll have done your writing brain some real good.

The amazing thing about this process of deeply studying the masters is that *nothing is hidden*. In fabulously written prose, every word is right there in black and white, laid bare for the world to see. Yet few people take advantage of the complete transparency of the artistry of great writers. (This is not to say that the *process* of creating such writing is always transparent, just the final result.)

The English language is a common toolbox that you can freely take from, if you study—and truly acquire—appropriate examples.

4. Do a few sample essays from the *Official Guide* (or the topic list available from mba.com).

Pick a prompt at random. Give yourself 30 minutes and type an essay into a barebones word processor, as described earlier.

Then do the Microsoft Word analysis (Word Count and Spell/Grammar Check). Get the statistics and keep them in a spreadsheet, so you can track your progress.

Now, without the pressure of time, analyze and rewrite each sentence in your essay. How could you have phrased your thought more precisely and more expressively? What words could you have chosen differently? How would you restructure the sentence?

At first, focus on polishing only the ideas that you were able to generate under time pressure. This way, the next time you have similar thoughts (as you will on other essays), the corresponding sentences will more easily and quickly coalesce.

Now look for small gaps that you could close by adding material. Could you bulk up any existing sentences? What additional refinements could you add as modifiers? Could you provide better navigation and logical flow with signal words?

Finally, look for big gaps and other wholesale alterations. Did you miss any key flaws in the argument? If so, which kinds? Write and polish sentences corresponding to these flaws. Is there anything you'd cut or otherwise change drastically? If so, what?

Do one essay per week, taking time between to read/recopy high-quality articles, so that you add to your treasure chest of expressive "bits" of English.

5. Learn to type faster.

The faster and more easily you can type, the less brainpower goes into typing—and the more goes into your thinking and writing. If you type slowly, then your brain runs far ahead of your fingers, and you lose your train of thought. In contrast, if you can get your thoughts down in near real time, you will simply write better.

Longer essays get higher scores, by and large. But that's far from the only reason to learn to type for real. We're talking about transforming your life. If you spend more than 20 minutes a day at a computer keyboard, the time you invest in learning to type quickly by touch (without looking at the keys) will pay off more than any other investment you could possibly make.

Take a touch-typing course. There are a zillion free resources on the Web. Google "learn to type" and see what you find.

Finally, if all goes awry on Test Day, there *is* an AWA rescoring service on mba.com. For $45, you can get your essay rescored; contact GMAT Customer Service. Be advised, however, that you are unlikely to see an increase. Only even consider rescoring if *all* of the following conditions hold:

- You scored a 3.5 or lower on the real AWA.
- You scored a 4.5 or higher on GMAT Write.
- After honest and thorough reflection, you feel that you wrote a much better essay than your score indicates.

Even then, your best bet is probably to retake the GMAT, doing significant additional preparation for the essay in the meantime.